Church and State Relations in Pauline Epistles

Biblical Hermeneutics Rediscovered

The Series as the name suggests will focus on Biblical Hermeneutics, i.e., literary works concerned with methods of interpreting the Old and New Testaments of Bible via different stream of topics like Literature & Poetry, Indigenous Philosophizing, Ethical response towards Ecology, Health & Healing, Science & Technology, Feminist Theology, Sociological approach towards Human Rights, Law & Politics, Arts, History of Ideas, Ancient Civilizations, Cultural Contiguity, Religious Cosmologies & Mysticism, Appraisal of various Theologians, World Peace & Harmony, Global Capitalism, Network Marketing, Cybertheology, Population & Demographics, Epigraphic Studies, Contextualized Education, and many others. We welcome a Mss. on any topic/s mentioned, whether they are original works, scholarly monographs, collections of conference papers, revised dissertations, or translations of historical documents. Through the Series we, the Publishers, are striving to put forward published works that may help Institutions, Academic Bodies, Researchers, Scholars and the World at large in furthering their respective knowledge and understanding on the concerned subject. We welcome your comments on our efforts and further suggestions on how we can enshrine new ray of analysing & explaining the written Texts through our upcoming books.

Biblical Hermeneutics Rediscovered - 21

Church and State Relations in Pauline Epistles

Its Implications for Religion and Politics in Mizoram

R. Lalrinliana

CWI

Christian World Imprints

First Published in 2019 by

Christian World Imprints
Christian Publishing & Books from India
C-3, Shop No. 14, Ground Floor
Wazirpur Industrial Area, **Delhi-110052**
cwidelhi2017@gmail.com
www.ChristianWorldImprints.com
Phone: +91 11 41526079

ISBN: 978-93-5148-364-9 (HB)
ISBN: 978-93-5148-365-6 (PB)

Printed in India.

Contents

Dedication

In Loving Memory of
my beloved father R. Sapchhunga
who entered into Eternal Glory on the
21st September, 2016.

Foreword

It is an immense pleasure for me to write a foreword to the book entitled ***Church and State Relations in Pauline Epistles: Its Implications for Religion and Politics in Mizoram*** which is the outcome of a sincere and careful examination of Paul's epistles to the Romans and the Corinthians, undertaken by Rev. R. Lalrinliana, a faculty member of Aizawl Theological College in the Department of Biblical Studies (New Testament).

In this book the author has mapped out the relationship between the Church and State from the setting of the Greco-Roman world and has beautifully brought to light the socio-political context of the Roman Empire. In the socio-political milieu of the text, the author skillfully unearths Paul's exhortation to Christians to be subservient to rulers and authorities acknowledging the sovereignty of God.

In today's context of politicization of religion, communal politics, questions regarding church and state relations, dissatisfaction and tendency of rebellion against ruling authorities and to what extent the Church should be involved in the State, this book will be immensely influential and effective in developing the perception of religion and politics, the involvement of the Church in political dealings and the prophetic role of the Church for the overall wellbeing and development of the society especially for the people of Mizoram.

Socio-political reformation can only be brought to reality through the Church and State working together in tandem and supporting each other. This book gives a clarion call to all Christians especially Mizo Christians to work for reformation in the social and political sphere in order to realize the Kingdom of God here on earth.

I have personally known Rev. R. Lalrinliana as a committed and gifted student who has obtained his B.Th. and B.D. degrees from Aizawl Theological College and M.Th. degree from United Theological College, Bangalore, and appreciate his scholarly endeavour and earnestly pray that he will continue to bring out valuable scholarly works in the days to come for the benefit of theological students, researchers and the faith community at large.

It is my sincerest hope and prayer that this book amplifies the wealth of knowledge in the field of biblical studies and recommends it to anyone who is engrossed in studying the Bible and unearthing its messages for the present context.

Rev. Prof. Vanlalnghaka Ralte
Principal
Aizawl Theological College
Durtlang, Mizoram

That the book in its original form is the thesis submitted to the Senate of Serampore College, towards the M. Th degree and is published with written permission. The candidate is responsible for the title, contents and opinions expressed in it. The original title of the thesis is "Church and State Relations in Pauline Epistles and its Implications for Religion and Politics in Mizoram"

Preface

This book traces Church and State relations in Pauline undisputed epistles Romans and Corinthians from the milieu of the Greco-Roman world. The researcher applied Social-Scientific approach as it agrees with the texts and the social world of the early Christians. The first century socio-political context of Roman Empire was influenced and maintained by the elite, the high class people. The Roman imperial ideology and theology espoused people to be more submissive to Roman Empire as it owed legal help and protection. Furthermore, the practice of the system of hierarchy in the Roman Empire won over the conquered people to become more submissive to the rulers and authorities.

The Social-Scientific approach with a critical-exegetical lens reveals that the first Christians did not necessarily foster resistance, but rather encouraged people to live under the rulers with obedience and submission to the ruling authorities for the welfare of the State. This shows that there was no idea of separation of Church and State in the early century as the Christians also enjoyed their privileged status whereas the conflicting situations within the Christian community at Corinth emphasizes the necessity of subordinating State as wisdom of God had to be motivating factors for the characters and minds of the people and the society. This book also highlights that Paul exhorts Christians to willingly submit themselves to the ruling authorities with their own conscience believing that the rulers are accountable to God. Furthermore, they are reminded that all powers and authority on earth are descended from God.

This book also attempts to bring out the need for the Mizo Christians to understand the relationship between religion and politics by bringing out identity politics, church involvement in political affairs and the prophetic role of the Church for the welfare of the State. The findings also show that there is an urgent need for the Mizo Christians to reform social and political life wherein both the Church and State should support each other in order to fulfil the *Missio Dei* on earth.

I sincerely thank Mr. Sudhanshu Kanda and editorial team of Christian World Imprints, New Delhi, for their immeasurable editing work and publication of this book. I also consider myself fortunate indeed to have had the opportunity to pursue my research work toward M.Th degree under the supervision of the Rev. Professor Dexter Maben. I am also convinced and profoundly inspired by their scholarly guidance and support of the Rev. Professor C. I. David Joy and the Rev. Professor G. J. Muthuraj. The research would not have been completed without their cooperation and constant encouragement. I acknowledge my heartfelt gratitude to all of them.

I also thank the Mizoram Synod for giving me an opportunity to pursue higher studies with constant support and prayers. My sincere thanks also goes to the Principal, the Faculty Members, the Library Staff of the United Theological College and also to all my friends who sacrifice their time for the completion of my research work. My gratitude also goes to my wife Rebecca Lalrinmawii, my daughter Hannah Laldinsangi and my son Timothy Laldinmawia for their unceasing support and prayers throughout my studies.

Thanks be to God the Almighty for His mercy and grace upon me, and to my Lord and Saviour Jesus Christ. To Him be the glory, now and forever more.

R. Lalrinliana

List of Abbreviations

AB	:	Anchor Bible
ABD	:	Anchor Bible Dictionary
AJT	:	Asia Journal of Theology
ANTC	:	Abingdon New Testament Commentary
Ant.	:	Jewish Antiquities
APHCL	:	All Party Hill Leaders' Conference
ATR	:	Anglican Theological Review
BAGD	:	Bauer, W., W. F. Arndt, F. W. Gingdrich, and F. W. Danker. *A Greek – English - Lexicon of the New Testament and Other Early Christian Literature.* 2nd Edition. Chicago, 1979.
BCE	:	Before Common Era
BNTC	:	Black's New Testament Commentary
BTESSC	:	Board of Theological Education of the Senate of Serampore College
BTF	:	Bangalore Theological Forum
CE	:	Common Era
Cf.	:	*confer* (compare)
Diss.	:	Dissertation
e.g.	:	*Exempli gratia* (for example)
ed.(s)	:	Editor(s)
EDNT	:	Exegetical Dictionary of the New Testament

f(f)	:	Following(s)
ICC	:	International Critical Commentary
ICNT	:	India Commentary on the New Testament
i.e.	:	*id est* (that is)
ISPCK	:	Indian Society for Promoting Christian Knowledge
Ltd	:	Limited
LXX	:	Septuagint
MNF	:	Mizo National Front
MPC	:	Mizoram Presbyterian Church
MPF	:	Mizoram People Forum
Mss.	:	Manuscripts
MTJ	:	Mizoram Theological Journal
NAC	:	New American Commentary
NBC	:	New Bible Commentary
NGOs	:	Non-Governmental Organizations
NIB	:	New Interpreter's Bible
NICNT	:	New International Commentary on the New Testament
NIDB	:	New Interpreter's Dictionary of the Bible
NLCNT	:	New London Commentary on the New Testament
NIV	:	New International Version
NT	:	Novum Testamentum
NTS	:	New Testament Studies
OM	:	Operation Mobilization
PNTC	:	Pillar New Testament Commentary
PR	:	Presbyterian Review
RMCS	:	Readings in Mizo Christianity Series
SATHRI	:	South Asia Theological Research Institute
SCM	:	Student Christian Movement
SPCK	:	Society for Promoting Christian Knowledge
TDNT	:	Theological Dictionary of the New Testament
TNTC	:	Tyndale New Testament Commentaries
Trans.	:	Translator
viz.	:	*videlicet* (as follows)
Vol.	:	Volume
v(v)	:	verse(s)
WBC	:	Word Biblical Commentary

Old Testament

Gen	:	Genesis
Exo	:	Exodus
Josh	:	Joshua
Judg	:	Judges
Isa	:	Isaiah
Dan	:	Daniel

New Testament

Matt	:	Matthew
Mk	:	Mark
Lk	:	Luke
Jh	:	John
Acts	:	Acts of the Apostles
Rom	:	Romans
1 Cor	:	Corinthians
Gal	:	Galatia
Col	:	Colossians
1 Tim	:	Timothy
1 Pet	:	Peter
Tit	:	Titus
Rev	:	Revelation

Chapter 1

Research Problem and Methodological Consideration

1.1. Background to the Problem

Church and State relations in the Pauline Epistles have been interpreted in different ways as there have been many theories and divergent opinions in understanding Church and State relations in Pauline Epistles. It has brought many into a dilemma and many scholars attempted to bring out their relation both in a positive and negative ways. However, a study of these particular passages viz. Romans 13: 1-7; 1 Corinthians 2: 1-16, 6: 1-11 from the perspective of religion and politics in the Mizo Christian context is still unexplored. Thus, this research attempts to investigate Pauline teaching of Church and State relations in Pauline Epistles with an attempt to draw out its implications to religion and politics in the context of Mizoram.

1.2. An Elaboration

The relationship between Church and State in Pauline Epistles is controversial among scholars as there has been different interpretations on the passages. Some scholars have acknowledged that for many years under the Greek and the Roman rulers, the Jewish people indeed enjoyed life and were protected under the privileges of a recognized religion.[1] They were exempt from the normal requirement to participate in the imperial cult and were allowed to maintain autonomy in religious matter.[2] N. T. Wright suggests that Paul was happy with the civic and imperial structures of the Roman government as the state was actually serving to advance the gospel, by its good governance, new roads, proper concern for justice and peace.[3] Moreover, he observes that Paul is fearless in announcing, and living by, a different allegiance before the rulers and he uses his Roman citizenship when it suits the demands of his mission.[4] Johannes Weiss also suggests that Paul's entertainment of the idea of the state could come about only because fundamentally he was not a Rome-hating Jewish fanatic, but a Hellenist and a Roman citizen.[5] However, some scholars suggest that Paul is supporting the Roman Empire of his fear of the rising problem that Jewish Christians might inappropriately support the growing tension between Jews and Romans which already existed in the community.[6] It was suggested that Paul wrote his letters to the Christians in the heart of the Roman Empire at a time when anti-Judaism ideology in imperial circles had begun to infect the church.[7]

---

[1] Ernst Kasemann, *Commentary on Romans* (Grand Rapids, Michigan: Eerdmans, 1980), 350.

[2] John Stambaugh and David Balch, *The Social World of the First Christians* (London: SPCK, 1986), 26.

[3] N. T. Wright, *Paul and the Faithfulness of God* (Minneapolis: Fortress Press, 2013), 127.

[4] N. T. Wright, *Paul: In Fresh Perspective* (Minneapolis: Fortress Press, 2005), 70.

[5] Johannes Weiss, *Earliest Christianity: A History of the Period AD 30-150* (Vol. II; New York: Harper Torch-books, 1959), 591.

[6] Douglas Moo, *The Epistle to the Romans* (NICNT; Grand Rapids, Michigan/ Cambridge, U.K.: Eerdmans, 1996), 729.

[7] Neil Elliott, *Liberating Paul: The Justice of God and the Politics of the Apostle* (Maryknoll, New York: Orbis Books, 1994), 190.

Emperor Claudius had expelled Jews from Rome in 49 CE[8] blaming them for disturbing the peaceful governance of the Emperor.[9] After a few years, there was Jewish resistance to Rome rule that led to a major revolt[10] which culminated in the destruction of the Jerusalem Temple in 70 CE. The revolt was partly the result of the poor and abusive administration of the Roman officials.[11] Moreover, taxation also appears to have been a long-standing irritant to the Jews of Palestine[12] as the Jews had paid land and customs taxes to the Romans since 63 BCE when Judea became a Roman tributary.[13] Thus, Pauline Christians at that time somehow came out with some resentment to the Roman rule.[14] Therefore, it is obvious that there were differing interpretations of Church and State relations in the Pauline Roman world.

It is undeniable that a good number of Mizo Christians maintain a negative attitude towards the state and revolt against any active participation in politics and state administration. In the Mizoram, where the percentage of Christians is 87.16 %,[15] many Mizo people are confused as to what extent Christians should participate or get involved in politics. Thus, it is a pressing need to bring out a biblical understanding which may be taken as a resource tool for the Mizo Christians to change society for the better. Hence, in view of the aforementioned interpretations, the researcher's attempt is to study the church and State relations in Pauline Epistles with the

---

[8] Seyoon Kim, *Christ and Caesar: The Gospel and the Roman Empire in the Writings of Paul and Luke* (Grand Rapids, Michigan: Eerdmans, 2008), 37.

[9] S. C. Mott, "Civil Authority," in *Dictionary of Paul and His Letters* (eds. Gerald F. Hawthorne, Ralph P. Martin and Daniel G. Reid; Leicester, England: Inter-Varsity Press, 1993), 142.

[10] C. H. Dodd, *The Epistle of Paul to the Romans* (London: Hodder and Stoughton, 1949), 200.

[11] Daniel Kroger, "Paul and the Civil Authorities: An Exegesis of Romans 13:1-7," *AJT* 7/2 (1993): 352.

[12] Kroger, "Paul and the Civil Authorities" 352.

[13] Kroger, "Paul and the Civil Authorities" 352-354.

[14] Dodd, *The Epistle of Paul to the Romans*, 200.

[15] http://www.census2011.co.in/data/religion/state/15-mizoram.html. Accessed on 27th February, 2017.

following method of research and to bring out its implications for religion and politics in the context of Mizoram.

1.3. Research Purpose

The purpose of this research is to explore Paul's understanding of the relationship between Church and State in the Greco-Roman Empire as found in the selected texts from the Pauline epistles to the Romans and Corinthians and attempts to bring out its implications for the religion and politics in the contemporary context of Mizoram.

1.4. Methodology Applied

This research will apply the Social-Scientific method in evaluating, examining and exposing the texts to find out the meaning of the passages. In order to clearly understand the text and its social world, the researcher proposes to use one of the methodological tools used by John H. Elliott 'sociological approach.'[16] According to Elliott, it is that phase of an exegetical task which analyses the social and cultural dimensions of the text and its environmental context through the utilization of the perspectives, theory, models and research of the social science. It also seeks to understand the texts in their social, cultural, historical, and literary contexts in order to understand the social institutions, the cultural values, and the norms of a particular community.[17] Since Social-Scientific criticism is not concerned only with the original meanings of the biblical documents,[18] this approach investigates biblical texts as meaningful configurations of language intended to communicate between composers and audience.[19] The exegetical study on the texts will also help the researcher to draw out a clearer picture in the Pauline understanding of church and state relationship in the selected texts.

---

[16] John H. Elliott, *What is Social-Scientific Criticism?* (Minneapolis: Fortress Press, 1993), 7.

[17] W. Randolph Tate, *Biblical Interpretation: Integrated Approach* (3rd ed.; Massachusetts: Hendrickson Publishers, 2008), 78.

[18] Elliott, *What is Social- Scientific criticism?*, 58.

[19] Dietmar Neufeld, "Social Science: New Testament," in *The Oxford Encyclopedia of Biblical Interpretation* (ed. Steven L. McKenzie; New York: Oxford University Press, 2013), 301.

1.5. Previous Research

A study on Romans 13:1-7 had been undertaken by scholars from different perspectives. Clinton Morrison's book *The Powers That Be: Earthly Rulers and Demonic Powers in Romans* 13:1-7 argues that human rulers and their angelic counterpart must be interpreted in the light of the person and work of Christ which is adopted from the interpretation of certain New Testament scholars in a systematic way. Robert H. Stein article in his *The Argument of Romans* 13:1-7 attempts to investigate the construction of the Pauline argument in Rom 13:1-7. James Kallas' work on *Romans xiii.* 1-7: *An Interpolation* tries to present the passages as an interpolation as nowhere else in his epistle does Paul ever discuss the state and Christian's relationship to it.[20] An article from *A New Context for Romans xiii* by Marcus Borg offers an alternative exegesis and interpretation which depends upon setting of Paul's words within the context of Jewish nationalism.[21] J. I. H. McDonald work *Romans* 13:1-7: *A test case for New Testament Interpretation* offers an attempt to pinpoint issues of the text at four levels in the interpretative process.[22] The article *Paul and the Civil Authorities: An exegesis of Romans* 13:1-7 by Daniel Kroger tries to solve the authenticity of the texts and with historical data or informative facts offer further insight into Paul's intended meaning in the text. Robert S. Dutch's work on *The Educated Elite on 1 Corinthians: Education and Community Conflict in Graeco-Roman Contexts* did an extensive study with Social-Scientific criticism as a model of reading Paul's text within the appropriate social world of early first-century Corinth.[23] All the above studies are helpful and significant for the study of church and state relations from Pauline epistles as it provides different view on the subject. However, in this

[20] James Kallas, "Romans XIII. 1-7: An Interpolation," *NTS* 11/ 4 (1965): 365.

[21] Marcus Borg, "A New Context for Romans XIII," *NTS* 19/2 (1973): 205.

[22] The propose level are as follows: text and context in Romans, inner logic and strategy, social reality and holistic exegesis. J. I. H. McDonald, "Romans 13: 1-7: A Test Case for New Testament Interpretation," *NTS* 35/4 (1989): 540.

[23] Robert S. Dutch, *The Educated Elite in the 1 Corinthians: Education and Community Conflict in Graeco-Roman Context* (London: T & T Clark International, 2005), 171.

research, the researcher will attempt to investigate Pauline teaching of church and State relations in the Pauline Epistles with a view to draw out its implications for religion and politics in the context of Mizoram.

1.6. Scope and Limitation

The scope is limited to the undisputed letters of Paul and an exegetical study will be done with the selected passage from Romans 13:1-7. In addition to this, an exegetical analysis will be done from I Corinthians 2:1-16 and I Corinthians 6:1-11 in order to have a wider understanding of Paul's attitude towards the State. After critically studying the selected texts following the research method mentioned earlier, the researcher will draw out its implications on the theology of politics in the contemporary context of Mizoram.

Chapter 2

The Milieu of Greco – Roman World

2.1. Introduction

This chapter deals with a brief study of the context of the Greco-Roman world where Christianity became one of the religions in the world. Rome in the first century stood as one of the most powerful countries as its empire extended from Britain in the northwest, through France and Spain to the west, across Europe to Turkey in the east, and along North Africa to the south. The Roman Empire colonized an estimated 60-65 million people of diverse ethnicities and cultures under which falls the territory and people around the Mediterranean Sea.[24] The New Testament writings came into existences where the Greco-Roman world was dominated by the Roman Empire.[25] Thus, in order to have a better understanding of the social context of the community of the Pauline writings, it is appropriate and necessary to explore the context of the Greco-

[24] Warren Carter, *The Roman Empire and the New Testament: An Essential Guide* (Abingdon: Nashville Press, 2006), 3.

[25] Carter, *The Roman Empire and the New Testament*, 1.

Roman world. This will also help us to understand the context of the origins of early Christianity.

2.2. Socio-Economic Condition of the Greco-Roman World

2.2.1. The Elite

The elite are the high-class people consisting of provincial governors, magistrates and officials who have a distinct relationship with the emperor. They received privileges through the Emperor and thus exercised, maintain and created power, wealth, and prestige through crucial roles in terms of warrior, tax collector, administrator, patron, judge and priest.[26] They fashioned the political, cultural and social experiences of the Empire and enjoyed an elevated status and quality of life.[27] The elite, particularly those who lived in the city exercised a number of advantages in the judicial system of the first century. They mainly included financial qualifications for jury service, influence over honorary magistrates and judges, and the importance given to social status in weighing judgments.[28] They also controlled public lands by their influence and bought cheaply the private lands of those whose families were impoverished by war or by the impossibility of living a normal life. The luxurious life style also desensitized these high-class people and at the same time discourages the lower class.[29] They were mainly based in the cities, and took control over the rest of the population who were mainly peasants and farmers, from whom the elite extracted a hefty proportion of their surplus to support their luxurious life in the city and the religious cult or cults that it contained.[30]

---

[26] Carter, *The Roman Empire and the New Testament*, 8-9.

[27] Judith A Diel, "Anti-Imperial Rhetoric in the New Testament," in *Jesus is Lord Caesar is Not: Evaluating Empire in New Testament Studies* (eds. Scot McKnight and Joseph B. Monica; Downers Grove, Illinois: IVP Academic, 2013), 44.

[28] Bruce W. Winter, *After Paul Left Corinth: The Influence of Secular Ethics and Social Change* (Grand Rapids, Michigan: Eerdmans, 2001), 62.

[29] Merril C. Tenney, *New Testament Survey* (Leicester, England: Inter-Varsity Press, 1985), 49.

[30] Philip F. Esler, "Palestinian Judaism in the First Century," in *Religious Diversity in the Graeco-Roman World* (eds. Dan Cohn-Sherbok and John M. Court; Sheffield, England: Sheffield Academic Press, 2011), 23.

2.2.2. The Non-Elite

The non-elite were the people consisting of about 97 percent of the population. They earned their living mostly from trade, artisan skills, and farming. Since most people belonged to this group, Christians also came under this umbrella.[31] The non-elite such as the peasants and fisherman, petty traders and artisans produced the goods that the elite taxed and tithed to maintain their position.[32] They were the people who lived at or near subsistence levels, making just enough to survive, with little hope of saving anything that would allow them to improve their position or provide them with a hedge against calamity. It was further suggested that of the non-elite consisting about 28 percent of the population lived under subsistence level, people who did not know from day to day whether they would be able to obtain those things that are necessary to sustain life.[33]

2.2.3. Imperial Finance

Even though Rome had gained great wealth through its wars of conquest, the principal source of income for the Roman Empire was taxation and its total annual revenue in the New Testament era was somewhere between 100 and 200 million denarii,[34] which was about 10 percent of the overall produce of the Empire.[35] Banking system was also introduced where funds were often supplied to the banks

---

[31] Carter, *The Roman Empire and the New Testament*, 10.

[32] Esler, "Palestinian Judaism in the First Century," 37.

[33] Mark Allan Powell, *Introducing the New Testament: A Historical, Literary, and Theological Survey* (Grand Rapids, Michigan: Baker Academic, 2009), 41-42.

[34] The Denarius is mentioned in several places in the New Testament where it is variously translated as "penny" or "shilling". It was calculated as the ordinary day's wage for laboring man in the East (Matt 20:2). Tenney, *New Testament Survey*, 59-60.

[35] James S. Jeffers, *The Greco-Roman World of the New Testament Era: Exploring the Background of the Early Christianity* (Downers Grove, Illinois: IVP Academic, 1999), 143.

by private individuals, whereas the bank only acted as agent.[36] Taxes collected were used mainly for wages and military expenses.[37]

In order to strengthening the imperial finance, the emperor promoted an alliance of the elite in the city, who ruled with Rome's permission and promoted Rome's interests. They merely held the wealth from land and trade, provided the personnel that filled various civic and military positions throughout the empire such as the provincial governors, magistrate and officials, and member of the local city councils. The relationship between the emperor and elite was complex as the elite benefitted much from the power and order.[38] The patronage relations among the imperial elite thus maintained public order and exerted control over the people.[39]

2.3. Religio-Political Condition of the Greco-Roman World

2.3.1. Roman Imperial Theology

According to John Dominic Crossan, Roman Imperial Theology is the ideological glue that held Roman civilization together. He further asserts that it is not to be understood as propaganda from an imperial top order to a colonial bottom ranks but as an extraordinarily successful advertising campaign supported by self-consciously "Roman" political elites across the entire Empire.[40] Warren Carter also said that Rome and its elite allies expressed their understanding that Rome's dominating place in the world was the will of the gods. It was propounded that submitting oneself to Rome was to submit to the will of the gods, and the means of participating

---

[36] Tenney, *New Testament Survey*, 60.

[37] Paul J Achtemeier, Koel B. Green and Marianne Meye Thompson, *Introducing the New Testament: Its Literature and Theology* (Grand Rapids, Michigan: Eerdmans, 2001), 28.

[38] Carter, *The Roman Empire and the New Testament*, 5.

[39] Richard A. Horsley, "Introduction," in *Paul and the Roman Imperial Order* (ed. Richard A. Horsley; Harrisburg, PA: Trinity Press International, 2004), 15.

[40] John Dominic Crossan, "Roman Imperial Theology," in *In the Shadow of Empire: Reclaiming the Bible as a History of Faithful Resistance* (ed. Richard A. Horsley; Louisville, London: Westminster John Knox Press, 2008), 59. See also MacMullen, *Romanization in the Time of Augustus* (New haven, CT: Yale University, 2003), ix-x.

in their blessing.[41] The followings points give us an ideology of some of the Roman imperial theologies and its related implications during the time of Greco-Roman world.

2.3.1.1. Imperial Cult

By the middle of the first century, most Greeks and Romans started at least nominally bowing down to the cult of emperor worship. The first emperor to be deified was Julius Caesar, acclaimed after his death in the year 27 BCE as the god of Augustus.[42] The worship of the emperor and his family, called 'Imperial Cult' began to be erected in the cities early in the reign of Augustus. The temples were typically located in a prominent place where mostly the elite men and women could gather for a festival, offer prayers and sacrifices on behalf of the emperor and his family to witness the mysteries, usually unveiling the images of the emperor himself.[43] The worshippers were given an elevated status and their outward faithfulness brought them prestige and power of the emperor and the other local deities.[44] As it was the case of the imperial cult, elsewhere in the Roman Empire and in Greek cities, religion was response to power, the ways in which society related to the powers that determined its life.[45] However, the emperor cult never became a new religion as such, rather a

---

[41] Carter, *The Roman Empire and the New Testament*, 83.

[42] Craig L. Blomberg, *Jesus and the Gospels: An Introduction and Survey* (2nd ed.; Nashville, Tennessee: B & H Academic, 2009), 40.

[43] David Nystrom, "We Have No King but Caesar: Roman Imperial Ideology and the Imperial Cult," in *Jesus is Lord, Caesar is Not* (eds. Scot McKnight and Joseph B. Monica; Downers Grove, Illinois : IVP Academic, 2013), 34-35. It was also suggested that the imperial cult originated in the province of Asia where the imperial cult and temple in Aphrodisias were established at the time of the formal deification of Augustus in 14 CE. See Bruce W. Winter, *Seek the Welfare of the City: Christians as Benefactors and Citizens* (Grand Rapids, Michigan: Eerdmans, 1994), 125.

[44] Nystrom, "We Have No King but Caesar," 45.

[45] Richard A. Horsley, *Paul and Empire: Religion and Power in Roman Imperial Society* (ed. Richard A Horsley; Harrisburg, Pennsylvania: Trinity Press International, 1997), 23.

supplementary glorification of the official religion which served the Roman State.[46]

2.3.1.2. Peace and Security: *pax et securitas/pax Romana*

The Roman peace called *pax Romana* was used to denote power to grant Roman citizenship to men of free birth. The emperors regularly granted citizenship to individuals and even to entire communities.[47] It gave the Empire freedom from warfare over time to the people.[48] This type of patron-client relationship owed the citizen legal help and protection from powerful enemies and in turn received the patrons respect and defense.[49] Thus, those who possessed *pax Romana* were entitled to special protection from the Roman government from accusation of non-citizens and exemption from the more extreme forms of punishment.[50]

2.3.1.3. Religion of the Greco-Roman World

A Greco-Roman citizen was a first or second century resident of the eastern Mediterranean who could speak, read and write Greek and was familiar with the early imperial Greek and Roman culture of the eastern Mediterranean region.[51] The Religion of the Greco-Roman comprised of a collection of Greek and Roman ritual practices such as oracles, magic temple attendants, philosophical schools and localized cults.[52] The religion was, therefore, neither simple nor private, but had a public character in its roles and function.[53] Since religion

---

[46] Helmut Koester, *History, Culture, and Religion of the Hellenistic Age* (Vol. 1 of *Introduction to the New Testament*; Philadelphia: Fortress Press, 1982), 370.

[47] Jeffers, *The Greco-Roman World of the New Testament Era*, 200.

[48] Blomberg, *Jesus and the Gospels*, 24.

[49] Jeffers, *The Greco-Roman World of the New Testament Era*, 192.

[50] Jeffers, *The Greco-Roman World of the New Testament Era*, 198.

[51] Lynn Allan Kauppi, *Foreign But Familiar Gods: Greco-Romans Read Religion in Acts* (London : T & T Clark, 2006), 16.

[52] Kauppi, *Foreign But Familiar Gods*, 16.

[53] Luke Timothy Johnson, *Among the Gentiles: Greco-Roman Religion and Christianity* (London: Yale University Press, 2009), 33.

was public, it was also necessarily political in character. Matters of religion were also matters of state.[54]

2.3.2. Roman Imperial Ideology

2.3.2.1. Societal Hierarchy in the Empire

The ideology of the Roman Empire was preoccupied with the challenges of winning the minds and souls of the conquered peoples in every possible ways.[55] David W. J. Gill beautifully explained the hierarchical system of the Greco-Roman society as divided into three legal groups. They are the *Senate,* the *equites* and the *decuriones.*[56] The Roman Empire was hierarchical in the sense that there was vast disparity of power and wealth between the groups. Carter observes that the division between the ruling elite and the majority non-elite made the living conditions quite uncomfortable.[57] Many cities were colonies, technically extensions of the city of Rome itself inhabited by retired soldiers. The political life of the imperial city was pressed to conform to the Roman pattern of life. The conquered areas had usually lost political rights and perhaps even material wealth. The conquered people were allowed to freely accept Roman ideology securing Latin rights and eventually citizenship.[58]

---

[54] Johnson, *Among the Gentiles*, 34.

[55] Neil Elliott, *The Arrogance of Nations: Reading Romans in the Shadow of Empire* (Minneapolis: Fortress Press, 2008), 25.

[56] The *senate* stood at the top consisting of some six hundred member, particularly drawn from several hundred families. Men from this group held higher magistracies at Rome, senior military positions, and the senior provincial posts. The next social group comprised of the *equites,* consisting of several thousand members, who came to the group through birth, as well as being granted by the emperor to freedman if they satisfied the property qualification. Both the *Senatorial* and the *Equestrian* wealth was based on land. The next group comprised of the *decuriones,* consisting of hundred most senior men, of varying of wealth, in each city of the empire. Below these group came the peasants, the freedman, and finally the slaves. David W. J. Gill, "Acts and the Urban Elites," in *The Book of Acts an in Its First Century Setting* (Vol. 2 of *The Book of Acts in Its Graeco-Roman Setting*; eds. David W. J. Gill and Conrad Gempf; Grand Rapids, Michigan: Eerdmans, 1994), 106-107.

[57] Carter, *The Roman Empire and the New Testament*, 3.

[58] Nystrom, "We Have No King but Caesar," 27-28.

2.3.2.2. Aristocratic Empire

Carter has pointed out that the aristocrat shaped the social experience of the Empire's inhabitants, determined the quality of life, exercised power, controlled wealth and enjoyed high status.[59] Wayne A. Meeks also interpreted that since the Roman policy was to encourage the aristocrats, an anti-Roman feeling was naturally more likely to be found among the lower classes than among the privileged.[60] The aristocracy continually reminded the others of their superior position by their suspicious consumption, by offering their clients inferior food and wine and banquets, and even by the fact that the law discriminated positively in their favor.[61]

2.3.2.3. Legionary Empire

The presence of military forces were an essential factor in the exercise of imperial power. The Romans established the empire initially by superior forces of arms.[62] The legionary empire exposed the coercive nature of the Roman army and the dominant means of coercion was the much vaunted Roman army of the empire.[63] A. Nicholas Sherwin-White said that the legions and the auxiliary regiments in the first century of the emperor were grouped in corps of three or four legions, supplemented by about the same total strength of the auxiliary units, throughout the military province of the northern frontier, from Britain to the mouth of the Danube.[64]

---

[59] Carter, *The Roman Empire and the New Testament*, 3.

[60] Wayne A. Meeks, *The First Urban Christians: The Social World of the Apostle Paul* (New Haven and London: Yale University Press, 1983), 13.

[61] Philip Francis Esler, *Community and Gospel in Luke-Acts* (Cambridge: Cambridge University Press, 1987), 172-73.

[62] Horsley, *Paul and Empire*, 12.

[63] Carter, *The Roman Empire and the New Testament*, 4.

[64] The Roman army consists of three main branches. The First branch were legionary army, which was maintained at the strength of some thirty legions. They were recruits only from the Roman citizens. The Second was a more varied force of independent regiments or auxiliary units of infantry, cavalry, and special troops such as archers and camel riders. These units were recruits mostly among the less civilized people of the Empire and they received a Roman citizenship as a reward of retirement after twenty-five years service. The third consists of three corps stationed

2.3.2.4. Agrarian Empire

The agrarian empire, according to Robert S. Dutch, did not simply mean 'agricultural' but referred to a pre-industrial society embracing both the rural peasant and the city-dweller, without contact with the soil.[65] The Empire's wealth and power were mainly dependent on land and consumed some 65 percent of its production. Paying taxes was compulsory and to not pay taxes was regarded as rebellion because it refused a recognition of Rome's sovereignty over land, sea, labor and production.[66] It was an empire of agrarian economy with land as the primary resource. The production of food was mainly from rural areas and the city people benefited and consumed the products.[67]

2.3.2.5. Patronage to the Emperor

David Nystrom argued that the emperor made himself unparalleled contracting the senators, equestrians and provincial elites. Social position depended largely on their standing in the sight of the emperor.[68] One of the effective means by which the imperial patronage system worked was letters of recommendation as it functioned as a significant instrument for the cohesion and durability of the ruling class of the Roman imperial order.[69] Thus, the ideology of benefaction and patronage was pervasive in the Roman Empire as it effectively

at Rome itself; the twelve or sixteen cohorts of the Praetorian Guard, which were the personal troops of the Emperor. The Praetorian troops were the spoiled special favourites of the Emperor, enjoying special rates of pay and terms of services. See A. Nicholas Sherwin-White, "The Roman Government and the Christian Church," in *The Crucible of Christianity: Judaism, Hellenism and the Historical Background to the Christian Faith* (London: Thames and Hudson 1969), 141.

[65] Robert S. Dutch, *The Educated Elite in the 1 Corinthians: Education and Community Conflict in Graeco-Roman Context* (London: T & T Clark International, 2005), 171.

[66] Carter, *The Roman Empire and the New Testament*, 3.

[67] Carter, *The Roman Empire and the New Testament*, 45.

[68] Nystrom, "We Have No King but Caesar," 32.

[69] Efrain Agosto, "Patronage and Commendation, Imperial and Anti-Imperial," in *Paul and the Roman Imperial Order* (ed. Richard A. Horsley; Harrisburg, PA: Trinity Press International, 2004), 107.

and simultaneously concealed the rapacity of the ruling class and naturalized the fundamentally unequal relationship through routines of highly theatrical reciprocity.[70]

2.4. **Judaism Under the Greco-Roman Empire**

Judaism under the Greco-Roman empire resembled in many respects the other surrounding religions. They were financed by wealthy patrons, they also had similar a organizational structure, and they had instruments for the assistance of the members in need.[71] While enjoying their living under the Empire, they had free exercise of their religion and were exempt from worshipping the deities of the Roman State. But some Greeks and Romans expressed a negative attitude towards them mainly because the Jews shared the accusation in which easterners in the Greco-Roman cities were held. Moreover, Jewish religion and customs were strange according to the Greek standards. In turn, the Jews themselves experienced the impact and influence of Greek culture, language, literature and customs. Although, there was some accommodation to the new environment, the Jews still maintained their distinctiveness more successfully than did any other people of the Mediterranean world.[72]

2.5. **Social Settings of the Early Christians**

2.5.1. Itinerant Charismatics and Community Organizers

There were two major groups that emerged in the earliest period of Christianity. They were the Itinerant Charismatics and Community organizers. The itinerant charismatics shaped the earliest traditions and provided the social background especially in the tradition of the words of Jesus.[73] The itinerant preachers forsook worldly desires and lived in a freedom from basic social responsibilities by means of

---

[70] Elliott, *The Arrogance of Nations*, 29.

[71] Johnson, *Among the Gentile*, 122.

[72] Everett Ferguson, *Backgrounds of Early Christianity* (Grand Rapids, Michigan: Eerdmans, 1987), 342.

[73] Gerd Theissen, *Sociology of Early Palestinian Christianity* (Philadelphia: Fortress Press, 1977), 10.

ascetic poverty.[74] These people rose in the social circumstances of the Palestinian region[75] and were the decisive spiritual authorities in the local communities.[76] The more they detached themselves from the worldly pleasures, the more they destroyed this world as if they had to work off their rejection by this world.[77] They were the people who upset other people by preaching the imminent end of the world.[78] Since they were regarded as outsiders, they found their chief support among people who were themselves living on the fringes of society such as the poor and the hungry, the weary and the heavy-laden.[79] They were called "disciples of the Lord" as well as apostles. However, Luke argues that the itinerant charismatics were not restricted to the twelve apostles.[80] Therefore, those who are usually categorized in this group were Jesus of Nazareth and his immediate followers, the "Jesus Movement."[81]

The Community organizers were probably the nucleus of the early Christians communities.[82] They provided indispensable material support for the itinerant charismatics.[83] They were the people who remained clinging wholly within the framework of Judaism and had no intention of founding a new religious community.[84]

---

[74] Gerd Theissen, *The Social Settings of Pauline Christianity* (Edinburgh: T & T Clark, 1982), 27.

[75] Theissen, *The Social Settings of Pauline Christianity*, 28.

[76] Richard A. Horsley, *Sociology and the Jesus Movement* (New York: Crossroad, 1989), 15.

[77] Theissen, *Sociology of Early Palestinian Christianity*, 15-16.

[78] Gerd Theissen, *Social Reality and the Early Christians: Theology, Ethics, and the World of the New Testament* (Minneapolis: Fortress Pres, 1992), 50.

[79] Theissen, *Social Reality and the Early Christians*, 51.

[80] Cf. Lk 10:1ff; Acts 11:27ff. See Theissen, *Social Reality and the Early Christians,* 62-63.

[81] Charles B. Puskas, *An Introduction to the New Testament* (Peabody, Massachussets: Hendrikson Publishers, 1989), 206.

[82] Some of the community organizers who welcomed Jesus are Peter (Matt 8:14), Mary and Martha (Lk 10:3 ff), Simon the Leper (Mk 14:3ff). See Theissen, *Sociology of Early Palestinian Christianity,* 17.

[83] Horsley, *Sociology and the Jesus Movement*, 15.

[84] Theissen, *Sociology of Early Palestinian Christianity*, 17. Cf. Gal 2:11f.

The Community organizers functioned in different groups in urban centres, like Jerusalem and Syrian Antioch and were well integrated into the political structure of the Roman world.[85] Thus, it could be noted that these two social forms i.e. the itinerant preachers and community organizers of the Jesus movement were both associated and distinguished by a graded pattern of norms.[86]

2.5.2. Urban and Rural Areas

The early Christian communities came into being in various urban regions of the Roman empire.[87] Most Christian communities mentioned in the New Testament were in cities.[88] Pauline Christianity was probably characteristic of the urban expansion of the movement.[89] Antioch, popularly known as the place where Paul centred his activities was the centre of political, military, and commercial communication between Rome and the Persian frontier and between Palestine and Asia Minor, and the home of a large and vigorous Jewish community.[90] It was the place where a controversy between Jews and gentiles first erupted within the church.[91] At the same time, it must be remembered that the sociology of early Christianity took it root in rural areas but spread primarily through the cities of the Hellenistic Mediterranean region.[92]

2.5.3. The Weak and the Strong

The early Christian community, especially the Corinthian Christians, came from the lower classes, stood in contrast to the few

---

[85] Puskas, *An Introduction to the New Testament*, 208-209.

[86] Theissen, *Sociology of Early Palestinian Christianity*, 22.

[87] Ekkehard W. Stegemann and Wolfgang Stegemann, *The Jesus Movement: A Social History of Its First Century* (trans. O. C. Dean, Jr.; Minneapolis: Fortress Press, 1995), 265.

[88] Raymond E. Brown, *An Introduction to the New Testament* (Bangalore: Theological Publications in India, 2000), 64.

[89] Meeks, *The First Urban Christians*, 10.

[90] Meeks, *The First Urban Christians*, 10.

[91] Meeks, *The First Urban Christians*, 11.

[92] Theissen, *The Social Settings of Pauline Christianity*, 176.

influential members who were from the upper classes.[93] They were petty bourgeois, manual workers and craftsmen, small businessmen and workers on the land, all of whom had a great respect for honest labour.[94] Christopher Rowland states that some of the disciples of Jesus themselves came from the lower strata of society and were described as uneducated and common men.[95] The basis for the disagreement that arose in Corinth over participation in meals was probably economic disparity between the rich and the poor in the Christian community[96] as the table fellowship was formed among the wealthy from which the poor were excluded.[97] It was evident that some members of the Corinthian groups conducted lawsuits against other members also implying inequality between the weak and strong in the community.[98]

According to Meeks, the lawsuits against members of the Corinthian groups implied some financial or mercantile transactions which had directly to do with different social levels in the groups.[99] Udo schnelle states to this:

> The 'strong' in Corinth certainly belonged in part to the upper social stratum, for whom it was possible to abandon traditional religious ideas on the basis of superior religious knowledge.[100]

Judith A diehl also asserts that a small group of wealthy families in Corinth controlled the city's power and prestige as the city was

---

[93] Theissen, *The Social Settings of Pauline Christianity*, 69.

[94] Martin Hengel, *Property and Riches in the Early Church* (London: SCM Press Ltd., 1974), 60.

[95] Christopher Rowland, *Christian Origins* (London: SPCK, 1985), 111-112.

[96] Ben Witherington III, *Conflict and Community in Corinth: A Socio-Rhetorical Commentary on 1 and 2 Corinthians* (Grand Rapids, Michigan/Cambridge, U.K.: Eerdmans, 1995), 28.

[97] Udo Schnelle, *Apostle Paul: His Life and Theology* (trans. M Eugene Boring; Grand Rapids, Michigan: Bakers Academic, 2003), 196.

[98] Meeks, *The First Urban Christians*, 66.

[99] Meeks, *The First Urban Christians*, 66-71.

[100] Udo Schnelle, *The History and Theology of the New Testament Writings* (London: SCM Press Ltd., 1998), 60.

more typical in its hierarchical social and political structure.[101] Thus, the religious and social reasons provoked conflict between "Strong" and "Weak" in the Corinthian Church.[102]

2.6. Conclusion

The history of the Greco-Roman world thus brought to light an understanding of the New Testament world in its context. This shaped different ways of understanding the world and the Empire as there are diverse and varied contributions to the origin of Christianity and explained the early period of the New Testament in a very detailed manner. A brief look at Greco-Roman world also helps us to see how and why the Greeks and Romans acted as they did in New Testament times. Therefore, reading the Greco-Roman context helps us to better understand the lives of the Greco-Roman people, particularly the early Christians.

---

[101] Judith A Diehl, "Anti-Imperial Rhetoric in the New Testament," in *Jesus is Lord, Caesar is Not* (eds. Scot McKnight and Joseph B. Monica; Downers Grove, Illinois : IVP Academic, 2013), 63.

[102] Schnelle, *Apostle Paul,* 196.

Chapter 3

The Understanding of a State in the Bible

3.1. Introduction

The concept of the State occupied an important place in the writings of the Old Testament and the New Testament. The idea of a State presented by different writers in the Bible indicated the manner in which the people of Israel lived under their rulers and functioned in the early period of Israel. This chapter tries to highlight some of the features of the kings and rulers both in the Old and New Testaments of the Bible and emphasis will be given to their socio-political involvement in day to day life.

3.2. The State and the Old Testament

3.2.1. Old Testament and Kingship Ideologies

The basic meaning of the Arabic root *mlk* is "to own completely" and may indicate a similar basic meaning of the Hebrew *melek*. It is an intriguing feature of Semitic languages that Hebrew had *melek* for "king" and *sar* for "official, prince" while Akkadian had *sarru* "king" and *malikhu* "counselor."[103] The term "kingship" in the Old Testament refers to the state, office, authority and dignity of a king[104] and the ideologies of kingship had come to Israel from outside, but had been modified to conform to Israel's own Yahweh-faith.[105] Kingship was the main pattern of political organization in the Ancient Near East. When it was understood to be part of the basic fabric of the socio-political order, the king was recognized as the shepherd of the people appointed by god to help society function in a harmonious condition.[106] The Mesopotamian idea of kingship[107] and the Ugaritic[108] and Babylonian mythologies strongly influenced the nature of kingship in the Old Testament.[109] Besides, the term kingship can also refer to rulers of states with varying degrees of size and importance, ranging from relatively small territories to empires such as the city-state of Tyre and Empires like Egypt, Syria and Babylonia.[110]

---

[103] Keith W. Whitelam, "King and Kingship," *ABD* 4: 40.

[104] K. M. Heim, "Kings and Kingship," in *Dictionary of the Old Testament: Historical Books* (eds. Bill T. Arnold & H. G. M. Williamson; Leicester, England: Inter-Varsity Press, 2005), 610.

[105] In the Egyptian mythology, the sun God *Re* withdrew himself to the heaven, he chose and appointed a human king to succeed him. The human king embodied both divine and human nature and was regarded as the son of *Re* by bodily generation. He was considered as the representative of God. He was the guardian of God-given law and must attend to justice in the land. D. Dhanaraj, "The Bible and the State: The Church and the Indian Scenario," *BTF* XXXIX/1 (2007): 144.

[106] Marc Zvi Brettler, "King, Kingship," in *NIDB* 3: 506.

[107] Throughout the different periods of Mesopotamian history, the idea of kingship reveals that kings were appointed and ruled by divine authority and were expected to create a prosperous, well-governed land. Heim, "Kings and Kingship," 611.

[108] The cultural heritage of the Ugarit kingdom was deeply rooted on compulsory military conscription, enforced labour for public projects, the duty to provide military equipment, the recruitment of female workers for domestic labor at the royal palace and the confiscation of real estate for king's use and practices associated with the monarchial system of neighboring peoples. Heim, "Kings and Kingship," 612.

[109] Dhanaraj, "The Bible and the State," 144.

[110] Heim, "Kings and Kingship," 610.

3.2.2. Pre-Monarchic Period

In the Old Testament, the people living under an umbrella of the theocratic rule of Yahweh[111] were completely involved in political affairs. Even though the civil authority of the nation of Israel was limited by colonizing forces, the people of Israel were never completely inactive in the arena of political affairs.[112] They entered the land of Canaan (The Promised Land) with the consciousness of being the people of Yahweh, the State achieved through Mosaic covenant which bound them to Yahweh in a special way. The covenant held them together and they were basically a religious community. They lived as tribes and were under the leadership of tribal or clan chieftainship. The people of Israel recognized Yahweh as the sole ruler of the tribal union and the idea of theocracy was central in their lives.[113] Therefore, an early Israel arose as an anti-hierarchic movement, socially in its formation by tribes and politically in its opposition to the payment of tribute, military draft, and state corvee.[114]

3.2.3. The Monarchic Period

It is clear that kingship was introduced after the people identified as Israel had been ruled by a series of judges, local rulers with charismatic authority who combined the function of military leaders and legal arbitrators.[115] In a monarchic form of a State, all the power and authority is in the hand of an individual who would establish a state-centered society by the rule of a dominating system and the office of the chieftain was endowed with divine powers, and exercising both priestly, prophetic and royal functions.[116] This monarchic form of

---

[111] John Bright, *History of Israel* (London: SCM Press Ltd., 1982), 155.

[112] Jose B. Fuliga, "Church-State Relations and Civil Disobedience," *AJT* 1/2 (2007): 476.

[113] Dhanaraj, "The Bible and the State," 142.

[114] Norman K. Gottwald, "Early Israel as an Anti-Imperial Community," in *In the Shadow of Empire: Reclaiming the Bible as a History of Faithful Resistance* (ed. Richard A. Horsley; Louisville, London: Westminster John Knox Press, 2008), 17.

[115] K. M. Heim, "Kings and Kingship," 617.

[116] Walther Eichrodt, *Theology of the Old Testament* (Vol. 1; London: SCM Press Ltd., 1960), 438.

government is the most common form of government in agrarian societies throughout world history. The king as the owner of the institution of the State was able to control the agrarian society and economy.[117] The people of Israel attained statehood as a result of the establishment of monarchy. The consequence of a statehood was the building up of a central administration, economy and army.[118] In Israel's history, though the first king failed to bring the expectation of both Yahweh and the people of Israel, the true form of God's rule came through King David, God's chosen king. Theocracy was then conceived as mediated through the human king, the chosen servant of Yahweh.[119] After King David, there arose subsequent kings who ruled the people of God in a different manners and the involvement of Yahweh in electing the kings could be seen though His prophets. After the establishment of monarchy, the people of Israel experienced dominations by foreign rulers over the powers of their kings. Richard A. Horsley states with regard to this:

> The Israelites eventually succumbed to domination by a series of empires, beginning with the Assyrians and Babylonians. Indeed, according to the book of Ezra and Nehemiah, the very institutional structure of Judea, in the south of Palestine, as a Temple-state headed by a high priesthood was initially sponsored by the Persian imperial regime. Besides maintaining local elites in power, the Persian encouraged their cultivation of indigenous legal traditions as instrument of imperial policy.[120]

---

[117] Whitelam, "King and Kingship," 40.

[118] Erhard S. Gerstenberger, *Theologies in the Old Testament* (trans. John Bowden; Minneapolis: Fortress Press, 2002), 23.

[119] Dhanaraj, "The Bible and the State," 143.

[120] Richard A. Horsley, "Jesus and Empire," in *The Kingdom of God and the New World Disorder* (Minneapolis: Fortress Press, 2003), 16.

3.2.4. The Perspective of the Role of the Prophet and the State

The Old Testament prophets played a significant role as mediator between God and the kings throughout the history of Israel. They emerged from every walks of life, who had felt the compulsion of Yahweh's word and who had often come to their vocation through some experience or call.[121] They were indeed specific, recipients of odd, psychic experiences, being visited by the supernatural in odd ways such as dreams and vision.[122] They exhorted, rebuked and rejected the kings for their behavior and injustice. They were intimately connected to the life of the State and were in direct contact with the kings.[123] Since the administration of justice was a royal responsibility that was exercised by virtue of the monarch's connection with the divine realm,[124] the prophets pronounced God's condemnation of the wealthy and powerful rulers for having forced the people into debt and control of their land, the very basis of their livelihood.[125] All the prophets emphasized that God is the sovereign Lord of the nations and that all human civil authority were only His instruments.[126] It was acknowledged that the prophets of the ninth,

---

[121] Bright, *A History of Israel*, 246.

[122] Walter Brueggemann, *Theology of the Old Testament: Testimony, Dispute, Advocacy* (Minneapolis: Fortress Press, 1997), 623.

[123] Prophets like Samuel, Nathan, Ahijah, Micaiah, Elijah, and Elishah were appeared in the 10th and 9th Centuries. Obadiah, Joel, Jonah, Amos and Hoseah are the prophets of the 8th century BCE. Prophets like Isaiah, Micah, Nahum, Zephaniah Habakkuk and Jeremiah appeared in the 7th century BCE and finally Exilic and Post Exilic prophets like Daniel, Ezekiel, Hagai, Zechariah and Malaki appeared at the last 6th and 5th century BCE.

[124] B. P. Irwin, "Social Justice," in *Dictionary of the Old Testament Prophets* (eds. Mark J. Boda & J. Gordon McConville; Nottingham, England: Inter-Varsity Press, 2012), 722.

[125] Richard A. Horsley, "Conclusion," in *In the Shadow of Empire: Reclaiming the Bible as a History of Faithful Resistance* (ed. Richard A. Horsley; Louisville, London: Westminster John Knox Press, 2008), 157.

[126] Robert Duncan Culver, *Towards a Biblical View of Civil Government* (Chicago: Moody Press, 1974), 88.

eight, and seventh centuries before CE reasserted the sovereign reality of Yahweh, which is not an addendum to Israelite self-delusion.[127]

3.3. The State and the New Testament

3.3.1. Jesus and Zealotism

The freedom movements during the time of Jesus was well represented in the struggles of the Zealots. The Zealots were Jewish revolutionaries in the first century CE. The term "Zealot" was the name of the radical party which led the defense of the Jerusalem, fighting the Romans for the freedom from domination.[128] The Zealots were the only ones who had vehemently opposed, even to the point of armed rebellion, the domination of the Roman empire over Israel.[129] It has been argued that Jesus was deeply involved in the politics of the time and that he started a religio-political movement.[130] One of Jesus' disciples named Simon is referred to as "the Zealot"[131] and the Zealots were the ones responsible for inciting the First Jewish War (66-74 CE).[132] Richard Horsley and John Hanson envision the Zealots as peasant brigands in contrast to more educated level of resistance.[133] It was argued that the chief priests and the prominent Pharisees who valued their social position did not want to anger the Romans and perhaps lose their favored status. In such a situation, the Zealot actively resisted this new aggressive approach to Rome, and soon a civil war erupted.[134]

Whether or not Jesus has an intimate relationship with the Zealots is still an unanswered question for many scholars. It must

---

[127] Brueggemann, *Theology of the Old Testament*, 640.

[128] Bell, *Exploring the New Testament World*, 38.

[129] V. J. John, "The Role of the State in Jesus' View," *BTF* XXXVI/1 (2004): 2.

[130] Albert Nolan, *Jesus Before Christianity* (Maryknoll, New York: Orbis Books, 2003), 114.

[131] Lk 6:15; Acts 1:13.

[132] Warren Heard, "Zealot," *NIDB* 5: 958.

[133] Richard A. Horsley and John S. Hanson, *Bandits, Prophets & Messiahs: Popular Movements in the Time of Jesus* (ed. Richard A. Horsley; San Francisco: Harper and Row Publishers, 1988), 214-217.

[134] Heard, "Zealot," 960.

be noted that he may not have supported the early use of the title "Zealot," but nevertheless support the continuing existence of revolutionary sentiments through the early first century CE, hence the relevance of such sentiments to Jesus days.[135] The revolutionary activity of Jesus has somehow indicated that Jesus as 'a political revolutionary' as Jesus did not reject tax collectors or Zealots when they came to him neither does he breaks off his relationship with the Pharisees, even though they were his opponents and at times he attacked them sharply.[136] There are a number of reference which can be related to the activities or conduct of Zealots that can be identified in the Gospel.[137] However, Jesus denounces the ideology of the Zealots who aspired to bring about political power over the ruling Roman Empire and tries to avoid the title "Messiah" for fear of being misunderstood by his disciples and others as a political king.[138] Rather, the objective of the politics of Jesus was the formation of a State based upon justice and righteousness.[139]

3.3.2. Pauline View on the State

In his epistles, Paul does not speak directly of the Christian attitude towards the State in the event of its becoming a totalitarian power. Rather all his theological convictions are strongly rooted in his faith in Jesus Christ as the one having absolute power over all powers.[140] Cullmann proposes that in order to have better understanding of Paul's attitudes toward

---

[135] Craig S. Keener, *The Historical Jesus of the Gospels* (Grand Rapids, Michigan: Eerdmans, 2009), 351.

[136] Martin Hengel, *Was Jesus a Revolutionist?* (trans. William Klassen; Philadelphia: Fortress Press, 1971), 28.

[137] The question of tribute money in Mk 12:13-17; Matt 22:15-12; Lk 20:20-26; the words of Jesus "I came not to bring peace, but a sword in Matt 10:34f. Lk 12:51ff; and presentation of disciples as 'armed' in Lk 22:35-38.

[138] C. Biakmawia, "Biblical Resources for Christian Participation in Politics," *MTJ* XI & XII (2005): 10.

[139] James Massey, "Inter-Play of Religion, Politics and Communalism in India," in *Inter-play of Religion, Politics and Communalism* (ed. Samson Prabhakar; Bangalore: BTESSC/SATHRI, 2004), 10.

[140] Dhanaraj, "The Bible and the State," 151.

the State, one should not neglect the passages from Rom 13:1-7, 1 Corinthians 2:1-6 and 6: 1-11 as these passages touches upon a specially important institution-the State.[141]

In Romans 13:1-7, Paul considers the authority of the state as 'ordained by God'[142] as they were directed and operated within the framework of divine justice by approving the fate of the good and the evil on the principle of retribution.[143] Herbert M. Gale also proposes that when Paul writes that the State s divinely instituted, he does not mean that it possesses final or supreme authority.[144] Paul does not in any sense, deny the State's right to administer justice in its own affairs.[145] Thus the state authorities, according to Paul, are ministers of God and exhort the Roman Christians to pay all their dues without any reservation. [146]

Paul in 1 Corinthians 2: 8 speaks about the State that "none of the rulers of this world understood it, for if they knew, they would not have crucified the Lord of glory." The limitation of the authority of the rulers is seen here in their wrong judgment against Jesus Christ as their inability to understand the wisdom of God.[147] Cullmann agrees that the interpretation of the "rulers of this world" as earthly political rulers or demonic invisible powers which stand behind all earthly happenings and use human beings as their effective agents.[148] In Corinthians 6:1ff., Paul orders the Corinthian Christians not to bring their controversies before the State's court of Justice. If certain case arises among them, they should refer the lawsuits and settle them among themselves within the congregation and not before the earthly rulers. This is due to the fact that Christians will one day sit

---

[141] Oscar Cullmann, *The State in the New Testament* (London: SCM Press Ltd., 1963), 49.

[142] Cf. Jn 19:11.

[143] Dhanaraj, "The Bible and the State," 150.

[144] Herbert M. Gale, "Paul's View of the State: A Discussion of the Problems in Romans 13: 1-7," *Interpretation* VI/4 (1952): 413.

[145] Cullmann, *The State in the New Testament*, 50.

[146] Dhanaraj, "The Bible and the State," 150.

[147] Dhanaraj, "The Bible and the State," 151.

[148] Cullmann, *The State in the New Testament*, 51.

in the judgment over those powers which now stand invisible behind the state.[149] The next chapter will discuss in greater more details how Paul's views of the state with an exegetical analysis.

3.3.3. The State in the Apocalypse

The Book of Revelation bears witness to the conflict between God's faithfulness and the Roman State. The socio-historical setting for the composition of the Book of Revelations seems to have been that of a severe persecution of Christians in Asia Minor, under the reign of Roman Emperor Domitian around 81-96 CE.[150] It is seen against the background of the religious conflict the Church experienced with the totalitarian State power which claimed itself to be God.[151] It pronounces God's condemnation of Rome and its empire and looks for the future establishment of a new world coming down from heaven.[152] The apocalyptic writer exhorts the followers of Jesus not to accommodate the imperial Roman cultural system, and to bear faithful witness to Jesus in opposition to the Empire's demands upon their allegiance.[153] The book of Revelation thus provides a paradigm of prophetic vision that identifies Rome's exercise of imperial domination as a sole super power accompanied by economic exploitation for the benefit of the metropolitan elite, and this vision announces that Roman empire stands under the judgment of God.[154] Since the Roman Empire was becoming draconic, Christians were no longer considered as part of Judaism and were no longer excused from emperor worship whereas the Jews were excused from the

---

[149] Dhanaraj, "The Bible and the State," 151-153.

[150] David Aune, *Revelation* (WBC 52A; Dallas, Texas: Word Books, 1997), lxx.

[151] Rev 1:9–under oppressed condition, Rev 2:8-9, 13-16- crisis faced by the Church of Asia Minor, Rev 2:13; 11:7- the painful crisis of the faithful, Rev 12:1-6; 13-17-the conflicting fate of the witnessing Christians and Political oppression chapters 13-17.

[152] Greg Carey, "The Book of Revelation as Counter-Imperial Script," in *In the Shadow of Empire: Reclaiming the Bible as a History of Faithful Resistance* (ed. Richard A. Horsley; Louisville, London: Westminster John Knox Press, 2008), 157.

[153] Carey, "The Book of Revelation as Counter-Imperial Script," 174.

[154] Horsley, "Conclusion," 181.

otherwise mandatory worship of the emperor.[155] In such a critical situation, the author of Revelation invites the faithful Christians to be strong in their faiths and even suffer and die for the sake of their savior Jesus Christ.

3.4. Conclusion

The idea of State is clearly embedded in biblical writings and presented in different methods. The gradual changes of political though of the people of Israel show the supremacy of God upon the other nations and their created orders. The presentation of the sovereignty of God pronounced by the prophets strongly empowered the minds of the people which resulted in the optimistic views of the welfare of the people. The New Testament writings also made significant contributions to the relationship between religion and State to the Christians. Jesus ministry to the outcastes, the downtrodden and those living in the periphery of society showed the necessity of Christians' involvement in politics. Pauline teachings of the State as found in his epistles and the State in the apocalypse thus helps us to understand the position of Christians in the midst of suffering and persecutions under the Roman empire and how to tackle the problems in such difficult situations to create a just and fruitful state and society in the world.

---

[155] Dave Hagelberg, *The Revelation of Jesus Christ to the Seven Churches and to Us Chapter 1-11* (Delhi: ISPCK, 2013), 9.

Chapter 4

An Exegetical Study of the Selected Texts

4.1. Introduction

The previous chapter discussed how the ideology of State came to the people of Israel and explored the development of the teaching of State affairs in the writings of both the Old and the New Testaments. This chapter deals with an exegetical study of Church and State relations in selected passages from Paul's undisputed epistles to the Romans[156] and the Corinthians.[157] The passages selected are as follows: Obedience to the rulers (Rom 13:1-7), God's Wisdom and the Wisdom of This Age (1 Cor 2:1-16), and Christians and the Law Courts (1 Cor 6:1-11). An attempt will be made to highlight

[156] There is a majority consensus that Paul wrote the letter to the Romans somewhere between 55 and 58 CE from Corinth. Arland J. Hultgren, *Paul's Letter to the Romans* (Grand Rapids, Michigan: Eerdmans, 2011), 3.

[157] The place of the composition of first letter to the Corinthian is Ephesus as Paul mentioned in 1 Cor 16:8. Besides, 16:6 indicates that the letter was composed in or near springtime, as Paul is awaiting Pentecost at Ephesus. This might be around late 56 CE or very early 57 CE. Brown, *An Introduction to the New Testament,* 514, 542.

how Christians were supposed to be involved in political affairs of this world and at the same time, attention will also be given to the responsibilities of Christians for the well-being of the people. The method employed for the study of the texts is Social-Scientific approach and the main emphasis will be given to the relationship of Christians to the orderly world.[158] In order to meaningfully study the selected texts, focus will be given on certain verses which have more relevance to the subject matter.

4.2. Obedience to the Rulers (Rom 13:1-7)

4.2.1. Translation[159]

> *[1]Let every soul must submit to the governing authorities. For there is no authority except from God; and the existing ones have been established by God. [2]The one who resist the authorities opposed the ordinance of God. And the one who resists shall receive judgment on themselves. [3]For a rulers are not a fear to the good work but to the evil. And if you want not to fear the authority, do good things and you will have praise. [4]For he is a minister of God to you to do good. But if you do wrong, be afraid, for he does not bear the sword in vain. For he is a servant of God; an avenger to execute anger upon those who practices evil things. [5]Therefore, it is necessary to be subject not only for wrath, but also for conscience's sake. [6]Therefore, also you pay taxes, for the ministers of God, they are attending constantly for this reason. [7]Render to all what is due, to the taxes, pay taxes, to the revenue, pay revenue, to respect to whom respect.*

[158] A number of references is found in the New Testament which deals with the relationship of Christians to the State such as Mk 12:13-17; Acts 5:29; 1Tim 2:1-2; 1 Pet 2:13-17; Rev 13. See Peter Stuhlmacher, *Paul's Letter to the Romans* (trans. Scott J. Hafemann; Edinburgh: T & T Clark, 1994), 206.

[159] Translation is from the researcher's own.

4.2.2. The Background-Hypotheses

Most scholars have agreed that the Roman Christians were in a difficult and vulnerable social-political situation. Their identity was ambivalent both for those inside the church and for those outside who would still probably have viewed Christian community within Judaism.[160] The early Christians also understood that normal conditions do not always prevail and that dangerous threats to the faith can arise in which obedience owed to God requires that the totalitarian claim of human authorities must be resisted.[161] Peter Oakes suggests that Paul's writing of Romans 13: 1-7 represents a pattern of fundamental tension inherent in early Christian attitudes to Rome.[162]

The early Christians' resistance to the Roman Empire during Paul's time have shown the relationship between church and politics in a certain manners. There was a belief that due to the expulsion of the Jews under Claudius in 49 CE, some Christians in Rome were compelled to conform or rebel against the Roman authorities.[163] Ben Witherington III asserted that Paul wrote this unit during the good years of Nero's reign, the time before Christians were persecuted as he wanted the Christian community both to be unified and not to have a negative attitude towards the Roman Government.[164] Ernst

---

[160] Philip H. Towner, "Romans 13:1-7 and Paul's Missiological Perspective: A Call to Political Quietism or Tranformation?" in *Romans & The People of God* (eds. Sven K. Soderlund & N. T. Wright; Grand Rapids, Michigan: Eerdmans, 1999), 167.

[161] Edward Lohse, *Theological Ethics of the New Testament* (trans. Eugene Boring; Minneapolis: Fortress Press, 1988), 136.

[162] Peter Oakes, "A State of Tension," in *The Gospel of Matthew in Its Roman Imperial Context* (eds. John K. Riches and David C. Sim; London/New York: T & T Clark International, 2005), 76.

[163] McDonald, "Romans 13:1-7," 545.

[164] Ben Witherington III, *Paul's Letter to the Romans: A Socio-Rhetorical Commentary* (Grand Rapids, Michigan: Eerdmans, 2004), 310. William Sanday and Arthur C. Headlam also claimed that when Paul wrote this Epistle to the Romans, the Roman Empire had never appeared in the character of persecutor. Rather, persecution had up to this times always comes from the Jews or from people riots such as the persecution of Stephan had probably taken place in the absence of the Roman governor. James, the brother of John was killed in the hands of the Jewish

Kasemann also commented that the Jews enjoyed protections from the Roman authorities and had the protected privileges of a recognized religion under the Roman imperial order.[165] Moreover, the Jews enjoyed an exemption from a law prohibiting the export of gold and silver which allowed them to send the temple tax to Jerusalem since maintenance and support of the temple cult was part of the Jewish history even before the time of the Roman Empire. Hence, the Roman legal system was attuned to recognizing the peculiar needs of Jewish religious system.[166]

Even though some scholars have suggested that Romans was written during the good years of Nero's reign, in which case Paul conceived of the Roman rule as beneficial and just. Thomas Schreiner rejected the proposal by saying that Paul was already an adult during the reign of Caligula i.e. 37-41 CE, and that he must have known the insistence of emperor worship, which precipitated a threat of war averted only by Caligula's timely death.[167] Moreover, Paul himself had suffered injustice at the hands of governing authorities in his own missionary works.[168] Therefore, the proposal of Paul's supporting the Roman state is naïve and somehow insupportable.[169]

4.2.3. The Context

Romans 13: 1-7 has traditionally been seen as a text that played a pivotal role in determining the various issues of Christians' relations to power, the state and the complexities of civic responsibility.[170] Daniel Kroger stated that Romans 13:1-7 is part of a section of Paul's moral exhortation that extends from 12:1 to 15:13 where Paul

---

king Herod. William Sanday and Arthur C. Headlam, *A Critical and Exegetical Commentary on the Epistle to the Romans* (ICC; Edinburgh: T. & T. Clark, 1958), 370.

[165] Kasemann, *Commentary on Romans*, 350.

[166] Kroger, "Paul and the Civil Authorities," 354.

[167] Thomas R. Schreiner, *Paul: Apostle of God's Glory in Christ* (Secunderabad: OM Books, 2001), 448.

[168] Acts 16:19-24; 35-40; 17:5 -9.

[169] Schreiner, *Paul: Apostle of God's Glory in Christ*, 449.

[170] Mark D. Nanos, *The Mystery of Romans: The Jewish Context of Paul's Letter* (Minneapolis: Fortress Press, 1996), 289-290.

exhorts his readers to live in conformity with their faith which is the saving gift of God's favor.[171] Especially in Romans 13: 1-7, it makes special mention that the people are to be subject to the authorities that are above them.[172]

However, according to Cranfield, this section is problematic as there is a lack of connection between the preceding section and its immediate context as it interrupts the continuity between 12:21 and 13:8.[173] For this reason, some scholars like James Kallas, F. F. Bruce and C. E. B. Cranfield consider the entire pericope of Romans 13: 1-7 as an interpolation.[174] The ideas that support this passage as an interpolation are-Romans 13:1-7 begins with a shift to the third person whereas 12:1f was in the second person plural; the passage seems unconcerned about eschatology as there is no reference to the presumption of an imminent ἐφσχατον was available in the passage.

Some scholars are trying to defend the authenticity of Paul's exhortation, for Paul is recognizing that the entire literary context of the passage is concerned about divine judgment.[175] Kasemann reviewed the discussion about whether it is an interpolation and concluded that there is no reason to dispute the authenticity of the text on either external or internal grounds. He holds the view that Irenaeus quoted it first in opposition to the Gnostic interpretation of the authorities as angelic powers means nothing in the face of the fact that some traditions which is obviously Jewish Christians were already used in 1 Peter 2:13-17.[176] Kroger assumes that there are some similarities between Jewish literature and the material found in Romans because Romans 13:1-7 seems consistent with first century

---

[171] Kroger, "Paul and the Civil Authorities," 345.

[172] Kroger, "Paul and the Civil Authorities," 345.

[173] C. E. B. Cranfield, *A Critical and Exegetical Commentary on Romans* (ICC; Edinburgh: T. & T. Clark , 1979), 651.

[174] The idea of interpolation is supported by prominent scholars like James Kallas, F. F. Bruce and C. E. B. Cranfield. See Kallas, "Romans XIII. 1-7," 365-374.

[175] Kroger, "Paul and the Civil Authorities," 347.

[176] Kasemann, *Commentary on Romans*, 351. No manuscript of Romans lacks these verses shows the authenticity of this passage. See Leander E. Keck, *Romans* (ANTC; Nashville: Abingdon Press, 2005), 311.

Jewish texts, as well as with older materials in the prophetic and wisdom literature.[177] James D. G. Dunn also supports the idea of authenticity of these verses as it clearly indicates the continuation of influence from Jewish wisdom and putting back basic categories at the beginning.[178]

According to Frank J. Matera, the unit consists of four subunits: 13:1a contains an initial exhortation that functions as a thesis statement, 13:1b-2 refers to a supporting argument for the thesis, 13:3-5 is an argument that exhibits characteristics of a diatribe, and finally 13:6-7 contains an application of the thesis to the question of paying taxes and revenues.[179] The differing interpretations and understanding of the text highly demands the detailed study which will further enhance the most probable meaning of the texts and gives relevant implication to Christians as has been already pointed out in the preceding chapter.

4.2.4. Exegetical Study of the Text

4.2.4.1. Obeying the Governing Authorities (v. 1)

Neil Elliott asserts that Romans 13:1 is the only point in the letter where Paul declares that his hearers' obedience to God will require their submission to the governing authorities.[180] Joseph A. Fitzmyer opines that Paul wrote this passage to the Roman Christians knowing that they have been conscious of imperial authority.[181] Douglas

---

[177] Jeremiah 27 is an example from the prophetic tradition's understanding of authority and divine vengeance. The book obviously believes that Nebuchadnezzar and the Babylonians originally received control of all people subject to them through the power of God. Isa 45-49 also manifesting a similar theme about God's activities. Both the notion that all authority is from God and the teaching that God works his justice through human instruments are similar to Rom 13: 1-7. See Kroger, "Paul and the Civil Authorities," 349.

[178] James D. G. Dunn, *Romans 9-16* (WBC 38B; Dallas, Texas,: Word Books, 1988), 758.

[179] Frank J. Matera, *Romans* (Grand Rapids, Michigan: Baker Academic, 2010), 294.

[180] Elliott, *The Arrogance of Nations*, 153.

[181] Joseph A. Fitzmyer, *Romans: A New Translation with Introduction and Commentary* (AB; New Haven and London: Yale University Press, 1993), 662.

Moo suggests that Paul tries to convince the kind of extremism that would pervert his emphasis on the coming of the new era and on new creation leading to the rejection of every human and societal convention including the government.[182] E. Bammel also argued that Paul writes this passage to combat all political inclinations among the Christians that he not only exhorts them to be loyal to the State but he gives concrete evidence formulae of the basic affirmation of the State, which could be understood by both the Jews and the Gentiles.[183]

4.2.4.1.1. πᾶσα ψυχή

C. E. B. Cranfield states that 'every person' that Paul referring to is those Christians who dwelt in the city of Rome and no one is exempt from the obligation to obey the words of the authorities.[184] Lohse argues that πᾶσα ψυχή[185] comes from traditional Jewish context which is used to denote a way of referring to every individual person[186] who possessed life or a soul.[187] In line with Lohse, Fitzmyer comments that πᾶσα ψυχή is literally translated from Hebraism as "every soul" which stresses the obligation of every individual.[188]

---

[182] Douglas Moo, *The Epistle to the Romans* (NICNT; Grand Rapids, Michigan/Cambridge, U. K.: Eerdmans, 1996), 791.

[183] E. Bammel, "Romans 13," in *Jesus and the Politics of His Day* (eds. Ernst Bammel and C. E. D. Moule; Cambridge: Cambridge University Press, 1984), 174.

[184] C. E. B. Cranfield, *Romans: A shorter Commentary* (Edinburgh: T & T Clark, 1985), 320.

[185] 𝔓[46] and several Western authorities prefer to use πάσαις instead of πᾶσα ψυχή to avoid the semitic idiom involved in the latter. Dunn, *Romans 9-16*, 758.

[186] Lohse, "ψυχή," *TDNT* 9: 648-649. A. Sand also used the same idea meaning "every individual person" cf. A. Sand, "ψυχή," *EDNT*, 3:500. Dunn also states that ψυχή is Semitic, as the soul is the centre of earthly life, and at the same time soul is distinct from body and spirit. See Dunn, *Romans 9-16*, 760.

[187] "ψυχή," *BAGD*, 2: 894.

[188] In some manuscript like P[46], D* F, G and in the Vulgate Version, "soul" is omitted and there is the simple imperative " be subject to all higher authorities." Fitzmyer, "Romans," 665. In some ancient manuscripts like 𝔓[46] and various western texts, the sentence begins with πάσαις ἐξουσίαις ὑπερεχούσαις ὑποτασσέσθε, where the verb is taken as a second person plural imperative "be subject to the governing authorities." In spite of those witnesses, other major witnesses like a and

Moo observes that Paul is using the word ψυχή[189] along with the typical Old Testament and Jewish manner to refer to the whole person but not one 'part' of a human being.[190] Dunn observes that πᾶσα ψυχή is semitic (כָּל־נֶפֶשׁ-kol¯nephes) with soul as the centre of earthly life, the lower half as it were of the πνευμα.[191] Robert H. Stein asserts that while the passage is addressed to the Christians at Rome, πᾶσα ψυχή clearly indicates that all people, Christians or non-Christians.[192] Thus, the words πᾶσα ψυχή 'every souls' thus makes no distinction between Christians and non-Christians, and he is not referring to a particular people but rather he is referring to a universal duty for the sake of well-being of the welfare of the people.[193]

4.2.4.1.2. ἐξουσίαις

In the Greco-Roman world, the local authorities were called ἐξουσίαι, whose task it was in their respective communities to exercise the authority of power of the state, and to enforce the law and maintain justice in the country.[194] The term is used for both religious and political leaders, and in the context of the Greek speaking Jews, it referred to the chief officer or magistrate.[195] In a political sense, it also refers to the bearers of the authority such as human authorities like officials, government whereas in religious sense, it refers to the bearers of the authorities of rulers and functionaries of the spirit world.[196] O. Cullmann suggests that ἐξουσία refers to both

B, Old Latin and Syriac version have the third person singular imperative, so that the clause should be rendered as "let every person be subject." Hultgren, *Paul's Letter to the Romans*, 466.

[189] Paul used ψυχή 13 times out of its 101 occurrences and it cannot be said to be his favorite word. See Leon Morris, *The Epistle to the Romans* (PNTC; Grand Rapids, Michigan/Cambridge, U. K.: Eerdmans, 1988), 460.

[190] Moo, *The Epistle to the Romans*, 794.

[191] Dunn, *Romans 9-16*, 760.

[192] Robert H. Stein, "The Argument of Romans 13:1-7," *NT* XXXI/4 (1989): 326.

[193] Morris, *The Epistle to the Romans*, 460.

[194] Lohse, *Theological Ethics of the New Testament*, 134.

[195] Nanos, *The Mystery of Romans*, 304.

[196] "ἐξουσία," *BAGD* 3: 278.

human and angelic authorities.[197] Referring to the understanding of O. Culmann and others, Witherington III has seen ἐξουσίαι as a reference to supernatural powers who were believed to be behind or in cooperation with the civil authorities. He further mentions that every other occurrence of plural ἐξουσίαι clearly refers to invisible angelic power. But such texts do not relate to civic authorities. But the context of Rom 13 renders any reference to angelic powers, as highly unlikely for Paul, who has nowhere shown or indicated subservience to angels or demons in his writings.[198]

There is a proposal that when Paul talks about ἐξουσίαι, he is referring to hostile powers, implying that civic authorities being God-ordained or at least divinely empowered and ordered. The most preferable understanding seems to be that Paul is talking about human power who can serve as a servant of God.[199] C.K. Barrett suggests that the authorities here refer to particularly the governing authority of the Roman Empire under which Paul and his readers lived.[200] Foerster also asserts that ἐξουσία denotes the power of kings or the authorities in the government.[201] Daniel Kroger points out that Dunn rejects the notion of referring to ἐξουσίαι as angelic powers on the basis that such views would be a contrast to Jewish nationalism at that time and collide against verse 3 where Paul uses ἄρξοντες and ἐξουσία in referring to earthly rulers.[202] The word ἐξουσίαις ὑπερεξουσαι is sometimes used to imply political relationships of power of kings and of authorities.[203] So also, the

---

[197] O. Cullmann, *The State in the New Testament* (New York: Scribner, 1965), 95-114.

[198] Schreiner, *Paul: Apostle of God's Glory in Christ*, 448. Cf. Tit 3:1; Col 2: 8-15.

[199] Witherington III, *Paul's Letter to the Romans*, 311.

[200] C. K. Barrett, *The Epistle to the Romans* (London: Adam & Charles Black, 1971), 244.

[201] Foerster, "ἐξουσία," *TDNT* 2: 565.

[202] Kroger, "Paul and the Civil Authorities," 358.

[203] The usage of ἐξουσίαις in NT is closest to that of the LXX. In the NT, it is used to denotes the power of God in nature and the spiritual world, the power which Satan exercises and imparts, and the power of freedom which is given to Jesus Christ and his disciples. Werner Foerster, "εξουσία," *TDNT*, 2: 562-575.

Greek phrase for ὑπερέχω literally means "superior authorities" or those in "higher" or "stronger" position of "authority.[204] It has also been traditionally assumed to refer to the institution of the state, and contextually to the Roman Empire.[205] Thus all the scholars agree that governmental authorities are intended here.

4.2.4.1.3. ὑποτασσέσθω[206]

This word has the clear sense "subject, subordinate," and in the middle or passive "subject oneself, be subjected, subordinate."[207] According to Kasemann, this verb stresses the element of divine order or control over all human affairs.[208] It is often assumed that the Greek verb translated ὑποτασσέσθω as 'be subject' means 'obey.'[209] In Romans 13:1, ὑποτασσέσθω is not precisely the same as obey, but rather means "accept the claims of, submit to."[210] Thus this verb emphasizes the divine order over the divinely established world for the sake of the goodness of the people.[211] It is possible that Paul has in mind the usual custom that officials praise and formally honor those who provide civil service for benevolence. It should be noted that the verses are descriptive, not prescriptive, although with overtones of the latter.[212] Therefore, this word expresses the notion of submitting to a superior.[213]

---

[204] Gerhard Delling, "ὑπερέχω," *TDNT* 8:524.

[205] Nanos, *The Mystery of Romans*, 297.

[206] 3rd person, singular, present imperative passive of 'ὑποτασσω' meaning 'to bring under control.' Its usage corresponds to that in the LXX. The middle meaning reflects the social structures of Hellenistic-Roman antiquity. R. Bergmeier, "ὑποτασσω," *EDNT* 3:408.

[207] Dunn, *Romans 9-16*, 760-761.

[208] Kasemann, *Commentary on Romans*, 351.

[209] Cranfield, *Romans,* 320.

[210] John Ziesler, "Paul's Letter to the Romans," in *TPI New Testament Commentaries* (Philadelphia: Trinity Press International, 1989), 310.

[211] Kasemann, *Commentary on Romans*, 351.

[212] Hultgren, *Paul's Letter to the Romans*, 472.

[213] Kroger, "Paul and the Civil Authorities," 358.

4.2.4.1.4. ὑπὸ Θεοῦ τεταγμέναι

Under the lordship of Christ, rulers are part of the divine provision in His creation.[214] This means that all the governing authorities are under the order of God's will and his determination.[215] Fitzmyer said that Paul is influenced by the Old Testament idea of acknowledging the Father as the source of all welfare, prosperity, and peace brought by human civil rule.[216] The use of the participle τεταγμέναι[217] is in a periphrastic construction and the perfect tense emphasizes the state of condition, "stand ordained by God."[218] Thus, the implication of ὑπο Θεοῦ τεταγμέναι is of an authority ordered by God.[219]

4.2.4.2. The Authorities are Appointed by God (v. 2a)

Dunn states that the clear implications is of a state of affairs, a structure of society, that brings to affirm that resistance is not only against God's order of society, but wasteful of time and energy.[220] The typical usage of ἀντιτασσόμενος[221] in the LXX is for resistance which is unavailing before superior strength.[222] Moo asserts that since God has appointed human rulers, those who opposed the rulers are in a state of rebellion against the ordinance of God.[223] The same word occurs only in Acts 7:53 where Stephen's address his end not as the decree of humans but through God.[224]

---

214 Ziesler, "Paul's Letter to the Romans," 311.

215 Schreiner, *Romans,* 682.

216 Josephus ascribed the same teaching to the Essences by saying "for not apart from God does anyone rule. See Fitzmyer, *Romans,* 667.

217 Perfect passive participle of τάσσω 'to draw up an order, to arrange in place, to assign, to appoint.'

218 Fritz Rienecker, *A Lingustic Key to the Greek New Testament* (ed. Cleon L. Rogers; Grand Rapids, Michigan: Zondervan Publishing House, 1970), 377-278.

219 Dunn, *Romans 9-16,* 761.

220 Dunn, *Romans 9-16,* 762.

221 Nominative singular masculine present middle participle of ajntitavssw 'oppose' 'resist.'

222 Dunn, *Romans 9-16,* 762.

223 Moo, *The Epistle to the Romans,* 799.

224 Delling, "διαταγή," *TDNT* 8: 36.

4.2.4.2.1. διαταγῇ

Delling states that διαταγῇ refers to God's ordaining person and the man who withstands the official authority ordained by God is in conflict with God's ordinance.[225] Dunn suggests that the word τοῦ Θεοῦ διαταγῇ is used here to characterize the state's power, which is given to the act of God's appointment.[226] When the rulers of imperial government issue orders, it is given this task by God, so that it becomes itself a divine διαταγῇ.[227] The verb that is following is the perfect ἀνθέστηκεν connoting a state of resistance.[228]

4.2.4.3. Rulers are not a Terror to Good Works but to Bad (v. 3)

4.2.4.3.1. γάρ ἄρχοντες οὐκ εἰσὶν

The use of γάρ indicates that Paul intends to bring out a further elaboration of what he means by a divinely ordained society.[229] Dunn states that though other Pauline interpretation used ἄρχοντες as angelic powers and heavenly beings, here it can means human rulers[230] who are desiring the good ordering of society because Paul stresses the generic character of the political situation.[231] Delling points out the fact that in a myth of Plato the ἄρχοντες are the ones who exercise a divinely willed supervision over individual parts of creation. They are cosmic rulers with specific spheres of authority.[232] Paul, according to Ziesler, is here implying that a good citizen needs and welcomes the protection of law and order.[233]

---

225 Delling, "διαταγή," *TDNT* 8:36.

226 The word διαταγῇ occurs once in the LXX (Ezra 4:11) and once elsewhere in the NT (Acts 7:53). cf. Moo, *The Epistle to the Romans*, 799; Dunn, *Romans 9-16*, 762.

227 Kasemann, *Commentary on Romans*, 353.

228 Moo, *The Epistle to the Romans*, 799.

229 Dunn, *Romans 9-16*, 763.

230 Dunn, *Romans 9-16*, 763.

231 Fitzmyer, *Romans*, 667.

232 Delling, "ἄρχων," *TDNT* 1: 488.

233 Ziesler, "Paul's Letter to the Romans," 312.

4.2.4.4. The Authorities Do Not Bear the Sword in Vain (v 4)

During the New Testament times, the sword was the symbol of a Roman magistrate's *imperium*.[234] Michaelis asserts that μάξαιραν is a "knife" used in circumcision (Josh 5:2) and in the offering of Isaac (Gen 22:6, 10) and a "dagger" or a "small sword" (Judg 3:16) as opposed to a sword proper (ῥομφαία).[235] John Howard Yoder asserts that sword is not used here as an instrument of capital punishment since the Roman crucified their criminals at that time.[236] As μάξαιραν is used as the symbol of the executive and criminal jurisdiction of a magistrate,[237] Paul is using μάξαιραν as the symbol of penal authority, the power to maintain law and order for the common good by obeying law of the society.[238] According to Dunn, the phrase obviously has in view the power of life and death being the ultimate sanction of government.[239] Likewise, Marcus Borg assumes that Paul is not thinking in general of using the sword as the civil government's ability to enforce the law, but specifically of the military power of a pagan government as a means of divine judgment.[240]

4.2.4.5. Subject to the Rulers is Mandatory (v. 5)

The phrase ἀνάγκη ὑποτάσσεσθαι[241] needs to be given attention. Metzger points out that on the basis of external support a majority of the Committee preferred the same reading adopted for the text. However, in order to simplify the construction of the phrase, a few

---

[234] F. F. Bruce, *Romans* (TNTC; Grand Rapids, Michigan: Eerdmans, 2000), 224.

[235] Michaelis, "μάξαιραν," TDNT, 4:524-27.

[236] John Howard Yoder, *The Politics of Jesus* (Grand Rapids, Michigan: Eerdmans, 1972), 206.

[237] Rienecker, *A Lingustic Key to the Greek New Testament,* 378.

[238] Fitzmyer, *Romans*, 668.

[239] Dunn, *Romans* 9-16, 764.

[240] Marcus Borg, "A New Context for Romans," 217.

[241] Present infinitive passive of ὑποτασσω 'to subject, put in subjection.'

witness, chiefly western omit ἀνάγκη and read ὑποτάσσεσθε.[242] Taking the context of Paul's Greco- Roman world to be subject to the governing authorities, places the Christian community within the larger sphere of humanity and grants that one can know what ought to be done in the civil sphere.[243]

4.2.4.6. People of God are Demanded to Pay Taxes (v.6)

4.2.4.6.1. λειτουργοί

This designation is an old one, composed from the Ionic word λειτος, meaning "people," and ἔργον, meaning "work."[244] The concept λειτουργεω is derived from the service to the community versus service of an individual, and its application is extended to include many religious functions of a priest or cult in Greek society, in the LXX, and in rabbinic Judaism.[245] It is also used to express a person of property who performed a public duty or service to the state in keeping with his own conscience.[246] Kasemann holds that λειτουργος carries the idea of secular sense of the authorized representative of an administrative body.[247] Although, the word is used in a purely secular sense of servant, whether of an individual or of a community, yet the very definite meaning which λειτουργος θεοῦ had occurred.[248] The authorities are "God's servants" or "ministers (λειτουργοί)." Arland J. Hultgren asserts that this word is used in both pre-Christian secular Greek literature in the LXX

---

[242] Bruce M. Metzger, *A Textual Commentary on the Greek New Testament* (London, England: United Bible Society, 1971), 529. Some MSS like 𝔓46, D, G and VL (*Vetus Latina*) version omit ἀνάγκη and read the present infinitive passive of ὑποτασσεσθαι as second person plural imperative ὑποτασσεσθε meaning 'subject yourselves." See Fitzmyer, "Romans," 669.

[243] Hultgren, *Paul's Letter to the Romans*, 472.

[244] Hermann Strathmann, "λειτουργεω, λειτουργία, λειτουργός, λειτουργικος," *TDNT* 4: 215-231.

[245] Nanos, *The Mystery of Romans*, 307.

[246] Harold K. Moulton, *The Analytical Greek Lexicon Revised* (Grand Rapids, Michigan: Zondervan Publishing House, 1978), 250.

[247] Kasemann, *Commentary on Romans,* 352.

[248] Sanday and Headlam, A *Critical and Exegetical Commentary on the Epistle to the Romans*, 368.

for civil authorities or persons who perform a public service for the people. Later on Paul uses a verb form of the term in its religious meaning concerning himself (Rom 15:16). But in Romans 13:6, the term is used for officials in the secular sense.[249]

Here, τελεῖτε is to be understood as an indicative but not imperative. Two types of taxation are mentioned in Romans 13:6 ὁ φόρος (*tributum*) direct taxation or tribute imposed on imperial subjects, and τό τελος, which included *vectigalia* and *portoria*, i.e., indirect taxation, customs duties and the like.[250] Here, the noun form of φόρους denotes the direct tributary payment, such as property tax or poll tax.[251] On the other hand, the two taxes such as φόρος and τελος are seen as in this manner. The former one refers to the tax paid by the subject nation (Lk 20:22), which involves direct payment such as the property tax or the poll tax. The latter word τελος refers to taxes that were levied on goods and were therefore an individual form of taxation. Sales taxes and tolls would be included in this category. Thus, Paul distinguishing between direct and indirect taxes is probably an indication that he had heard about the tension over taxes in Rome[252] and the abuses of indirect taxation was causing increasing unrest within the capital at that time.[253]

4.2.4.7. Pay to All What is Due to Them (v.7)

It was known that the Jewish kingdom had paid land and custom taxes to the Roman government since 63 BCE, when Judea became a Roman Tributary.[254] During the time of Quirinius, the legate of Syria conducted the census and imposed the *tributus capitis*, a direct tax of each adult male resident.[255] The practice of paying tax was also seen

---

[249] Hultgren, *Paul's Letter to the Romans,* 473.

[250] McDonald, "*Romans* 13. 1-7," 546.

[251] Fitzmyer, *Romans*, 668.

[252] Thomas R. Schreiner, *Romans* (Grand Rapids, Michigan: Baker Academic, 1998), 686.

[253] James D. G. Dunn, *The Theology of Paul the Apostle* (Grand Rapids, Michigan/Cambridge, U. K.: Eerdmans, 1998), 675.

[254] E Mary Smallwood, *The Jews Under Roman Rule* (Leiden: Brill, 1981), 150.

[255] Cf. Lk 2:2.

during the Jesus movement as found in Luke 20:22 and in Matthew 17:24-27. Here the imperative of paying what is due goes beyond just money to respect and honor as well.[256] The word ἀπόδοτε[257] πᾶσιν τάς ὀπφειλάς reflects the words of Jesus in Luke 20:25 as "pay to Caesar the things of Caesar."[258] The dues are not merely those pertaining to taxes but include the debts of veneration and honor.[259]

4.2.5. Theological Implication

Romans 13: 1-7 is not simply a theoretical, rather it is an universally unchangeable theology of the state.[260] Paul is speaking of human government in terms of an ideal.[261] Paul exhorts Christians in Romans to adopt a practical attitude of obedience and at the same time urges the Roman Christians to submit themselves to the governing authorities whom God had ordained for them. His expression in Romans 13:1-7 exhibits the common Jewish belief that God can use all the earthly authority, all governments and all nations to carry out His divine purposes.[262] He boldly suggests that in the matter of exercising power and authority of the rulers towards the people whom they were serving, the powers were not their own, but came from God. To resist them in the exercise of their God-given responsibility is to resist God and so to incur his judgment and wrath. Therefore, it is clear from the above analysis that submission to political authority should be motivated not simply because of the fear of retribution but from a good conscience which is one of the purposes of creating human beings. But, care should be given to the text that if it is taken out of context and used as absolute word that Christians may undoubtedly comply with the governing authorities

---

[256] Witherington III, *Paul's Letter to the Romans*, 315.

[257] 2nd person, plural, aorist imperative of αποδίδωμι 'to pay back.'

[258] Schreiner, *Romans,* 686.

[259] John Murray, *The Epistle to the Romans* (NLCNT; London: Marshall, Morgan & Scott, 1960), 155-156.

[260] Towner, " *Romans* 13:1-7 and Paul's Missiological Perspective," 169.

[261] James E. Edwards, "Romans," in *Understanding the Bible Commentary Series* (Grand Rapids, Michigan: Baker Books, 1992), 304-305.

[262] Kroger, "Paul and the Civil Authorities," 358.

no matter what is being demanded. Every obligation and duty must be in line with the teaching of the Scripture and Christians should also be bold enough to tackle certain obstacles that can devalue one's own commitment to the living God.

4.3. God's Wisdom and the Wisdom of This Age (1 Cor 2:1-16)

4.3.1. Translation[263]

[1]And I come to you brothers, I came not with excellence of
speech or of wisdom, announcing to you the testimony of God.
[2]for I decided to know nothing among you except Jesus Christ,
and having been crucified. [3]And I was with you in weakness
and fear, and in much trembling. [4]And my speech and my
preaching was not human wisdom and persuasive words, but
in demonstration of the Spirit and of power. [5]In order that
your faith may not be in the wisdom of man but in the power
of God. [6]But we speak the wisdom among the perfect ones,
neither the wisdom of this world, nor the rulers of this world,
who are coming to nothing. [7]But we speak the wisdom of God
in a mystery, that has been hidden and that God destined
for our glory before the world. [8]Which none of the rulers of
this world understood it, for if they knew, they would not
have crucified the Lord of glory. [9]But, as it has been written,
"Things which no eye has seen and no ear heard, and the heart
of no man came up, the things which God has prepared for
those who love him. [10]But God has revealed to us through the
spirit, for the Spirit searches all things, even the deep things
of God. [11]For what man knows the things of a man except
the spirit of a man in him? So also the things of God, no one
has known except the Spirit of God. [12]And we received the
spirit not of the world, but the Spirit from God in order that
we might know the things that are freely given to us by God.
[13]Which things also we speak not in the world, which is taught
in the words of human wisdom, but which the Spirit taught,
comparing spiritual things with spiritual. [14]But a natural

[263] Translation is from the researcher's own.

man do not receives the things of the Spirit of God, for they are foolishness to him, neither he cannot know, because they are spiritually discern.[15] *But the spiritual man discern all things, yet he himself is discern by no one.*[16] *For who have known the mind of the Lord that he may instruct him? But we have the mind of Christ.*

4.3.2. Introduction

This section contains a second illustration of Paul's argument, returning to his own manner of preaching without persuasive wisdom, with which he began the whole discussion in 1:17.[264] Paul states plainly the rhetorical strategy he resolved on when he came to Corinth, which was to evade "sublime words or wisdom" that is to avoid Sophistic or ornamental rhetoric, and perhaps to avoid drawing on the various Greco-Roman philosophies of the day in his initial preaching in Corinth. The Corinthians[265] associated "wisdom" in the form of a rhetorical eloquence with their goal in life. Reference to mysteries and their different grades are mentioned in the Sophists writings and Paul claims that he can convey mysteries in such a context. But he concluded that only the mature are ready for such things and the Corinthians are yet not mature.[266]

4.3.3. The Socio-Political Background

The socio-political context of Corinth[267] within which Paul lived and wrote the letter was composed of a mix of religions and cultures

[264] Richard A. Horsley, *1 Corinthians* (Nashville: Abingdon Press, 1998), 53.

[265] The number of writing of Paul letters to Corinthians is under dispute. According to C. K. Barrett, Paul wrote four letters to Corinth . The first has been lost, unless a part of it is preserved in 2 Cor 6:14-7:1. The second consists of what we call 1 Corinthians. The third has been partially preserved in 2 Cor 10-13, and finally the fourth is contained in 2 Cor 1-9 excluding 6:14-7:1. Barrett, *Essays on Paul,* 2.

[266] Witherington III, *Conflict & Community in Corinth*, 121.

[267] The city of Corinth was rebuild in 44 BCE as a Roman colony by Julius Caesar with a mixture of Roman settlement in the Greek cultural context with a sizeable Jewish population. These represented the linking of at least three cultures, languages and religions. During Paul's period, Corinth became an important trade

that can best be understood as multicultural. This was especially true in the writings of Paul to Corinthians, which represented a narrow slice of life in the Greco-Roman world.[268] Paul's theological principle has started at the end of chapter saying that he is not relying upon eloquence or wisdom.[269] He believes that his theological convictions should be expressed in the life of the Church.[270] His letter to the Corinthians marks the beginning of Christian "casuitry' in the true sense of the term i.e. the application of Christian principles to special cases and particular problems arising out of private life and church situation, such as sex, social ties, discipline and worship.[271] The broad context within which Paul writes to the Corinthians has several factors. Throughout the Mediterranean world, the political structure of the Roman Empire, the cultural traditions of Greece, and the language and religious customs of the various regions may be regarded as different layers of socialization, one placed on top of another as a result of certain historical events.[272]

4.3.4. The Context

The main motives of Paul's ideas in 1 Corinthians 2: 1-16 is to show them the folly of their present fascination with wisdom, which has

---

and transportation centre. The city was decorated with gymnasium, an arrays of temples, and a number of public baths, and it was also host to the Isthmian Games, which was celebrated every two years. See, Cornelia Cyss Crocker, Reading 1 Corinthians in the Twenty-First Century (New York/London: T & T Clark International, 2004), 13.

[268] Crocker, *Reading 1 Corinthians in the Twenty-First Century,* 13.

[269] C. K. Barrett, *The First Epistle to the Corinthians* (BNTC 2nd ed.; London: A & C Black, 1968), 62.

[270] Barrett, *Essays on Paul* (Louisville: Westminster John Knox Press, 1982) 1.

[271] James Moffatt, *The First Epistle of Paul to the Corinthians* (London: Hodder and Stoughton, 1938), xxvii.

[272] Corinth was settled mostly by freedmen and by veterans of the Roman army, an interesting and rather competitive social climate existed with space for ambitious individuals to advance both economically and politically. Categories from cultural anthropology have been utilized to discuss the issue of slavery, of hierarchy, and of division between rich and poor in terms of honor and shame, and of patron and client relationship. Crocker, *Reading 1 Corinthians in the Twenty-First Century,* 11-14.

inherent self-sufficiency and self-congratulatory tones. Even the preacher whom God used to bring them faith had rejected self-reliance.[273] In this passage there is a shift from the first person singular in 2:1-5 to the first person plural in 2:6-16 along with what some perceive as differences in content from the surrounding context that has led to various suggestions regarding its origin and purposes.[274] Thus, 1 Corinthians 2:1-16 is the response of Paul to the Corinthians after he received reports from Chloe that the Corinthians were boasting over spiritual leadership. Paul boldly responded to them that the cross of Christ was what made the people significant and was the demonstration of God's wisdom and power.[275]

4.3.5. Exegetical Study of the Text

4.3.5.1. The Wisdom of God and Paul's Exemplary Pattern from the Founding Days (vv. 1-5)

In 2 Corinthians 2:1-5 Paul describes the content, manner and the result of his preaching during the time establishing the Corinthian church. He describes his ministry among them as a ministry that exemplifies the wisdom of God. He came to Corinth to preach Christ not with highly sophisticated wisdom and intellectual manner, but rather as one bearing witness to Christ crucified.[276]

---

[273] Gordon D. Fee, *The First Epistles to the Corinthians* (Grand Rapids, Michigan: Eerdmans, 1988), 90-91.

[274] Some proposes that this section non-Pauline and was inserted by an editor at a later time after the original composition. Besides, Ellis suggests that 1 Cor 2:6-16 is a pre-formed exposition created within a Pauline group and adapted by Paul into its present context. Furthermore, others think Paul gives his own exposition of true wisdom from God, but, in doing so, he likely takes up concepts and phraseology in Corinth that account for the unique language. See Mark Taylor, *1 Corinthians* (NAC; Tennessee, Nashville: B & H Publishing Group, 2014), 84.

[275] Andrew B. Spurgeon, *1 Corinthians: An Exegetical and Contextual Commentary* (ICNT; Bangalore: Primalogue Publishing Media Private Limited, 2012), 29.

[276] Taylor, *1 Corinthians*, 77-78.

4.3.5.1.1. μυστήριον[277]

Bornkamm asserts that the term μυστήριον means κηρύσσειν χριστόν ἐωσταυρωμένον "preaching Christ Crucified."[278] Bruce asserts that both in the Qumran and in the New Testament, a mystery is commonly used to express some aspects of God's eschatological purpose, though obscure in the past, is now revealed by a further revelation. This mystery was fulfilled in the form of the eschatological purpose through Jesus Christ.[279] Paul's use of the context is that the term "mystery" is used as the revelatory dimension of Christian proclamation. He continued to express this in 2:6-16 with particular emphasis on the Spirit as the necessary means of revelation.[280] The faith of the Corinthians is also grounded in God's power, not in human wisdom or performance or status associated with sophisticated speech.[281] Paul has shown the Corinthians that God is infinitely more powerful than earthly human rulers, however wise or clever they might be by human standards.[282]

---

[277] There is textual variant in v.1 with regards to this reading as whether μυστήριον or μαρτύριον. In the Pauline corpus, the term μυστήριον is firmly connected with the *kerygma* of Christ whereas μmartuvrion is introduces as witness to do something, occasionally in an active sense. Some ancient manuscript say "Testimony of God" instead of "mystery of God." For Metzger, the evidence for "mystery" is stronger than for "testimony". But in some writings "testimony" is the reading of many important MSS. The proposal that made preferable to "testimony" is that because "testimony" is more suitable to the initial proclamation of the Gospel, whereas "mystery" suggests the wisdom Paul was able to speak among mature Christians. Bornkammm, "μυστήριον," *TDNT* 4:819; See also Metzger, *A Textual Commentary on New Testament Greek*, 545; C.K. Barrett, *The First Epistle to the Corinthians* (London: Adam and Charles Black, 1968), 62.

[278] G. Bornkamm, "μmυστήριον," *TDNT* 4: 819 .

[279] F. F. Bruce, *1 and 2 Corinthians* (NCB; London: Oliphant's, 1971), 38.

[280] Taylor, *1 Corinthians*, 80.

[281] J. Paul Sampley, "The First Letter to the Corinthians," in *The New Interpreter's Bible: A Commentary in Twelve Volumes.* Vol. X (Nashville: Abingdon Press, 2002), 817.

[282] Margareth E. Thrall, *The First and Second Letters of Paul to the Corinthians* (Cambridge: Cambridge University Press, 1965), 23.

4.3.5.1.2. ἐν ἀσθενείᾳ και ἐν φόβῳ καί ἐν τρόμῳ πολλῷ

Paul references of "weakness" (ἐν ἀσθενείᾳ) and "fear and trembling" (ἐν φόβῳ καί ἐν τρόμῳ πολλῷ) often occur in the LXX,[283] which is used to express the dread that people are to sense in the presence of God and his activity in the world.[284] Showing himself to the hearers, Paul was not an impressive speaker, but in his writing, which always reads like speech has genuine eloquence, and for all its common touch and occasional Semitic structure rises to the height of the Greek prose.[285] Ben Witherington III suggested that Paul's φόβῳ καί τρόμῳ may mean whether physical appearance, a weak voice, lack of training in declamation, or inadequate rhetoric delivery, all of his performance did not come across as rhetorically adept. The real complaint that Paul may have is that he was not arrogant in his presentation or did not engage in boasting, unlike the sophists.[286] Thus, ἀσθενείᾳ "weakness" may likely refer to some observable physical condition.[287] In many places presented in his writings, there was a genuine correspondence between his own personal weaknesses and his gospel. He often mentions related words like "weakness of God" (1:25), the story of a crucified Messiah (v. 2). His word ἀσθενείᾳ served as a further visible demonstration of the same message, but even more to demonstrate that the message was of divine, not human origin. Thus Paul regularly glories in his weaknesses. This does not mean that he enjoyed ill health, but because they were a strong evidence that the power was of God and not of himself.[288] For Taylor, weakness could imply a physical ailment or any number of things such as poverty, laboring to support

---

[283] Exo 15:16; Isa 19:16. Some have suggested that these expressions may have been related to his ongoing illness of thorn in the flesh or it may be a kind of admission that Paul came as one who was nervous and somewhat intimidated by the task set before him in Corinth. Witherington III, *Conflict & Community in Corinth*, 123.

[284] Fee, *The First Epistles to the Corinthians*, 93-94.

[285] Barrett, *The First Epistle to the Corinthians*, 64.

[286] Witherington III, *Conflict & Community in Corinth*, 124.

[287] Stahlin, "ἀσθενείᾳ," *TDNT* 1:491.

[288] Fee, *The First Epistles to the Corinthians*, 93.

oneself in ministry, or persecution.[289] Fee suggests Paul's fear as he likely referring to something which is observable in the physical condition. He further asserts that it reflects the general picture given in Acts 18:9-11, where Paul seems to be overwhelmed by the task of evangelizing in Corinth city.[290] Leon Morris observes that Paul's fear was primarily of God rather than of his fellow human beings.[291] Taking the assumptions of the above, it is probable that it refers to his own experiences in preaching rather than the task of evangelizing the gospel of Jesus Christ.

4.3.5.1.3. Preaching with Manifestation of Spirit and Power (vv. 4-5)

Looking back to v.1, there is no any difference in meaning between λόγος "message" and κήρυγμα "preaching" as it is a case of rhetorical duplication.[292] Still, various explanations have been given to the difference between λόγος and κήρυγμα and it is clear that to make the former 'private conversation' and the latter 'public preaching' is not satisfactory.[293] Paul employs both terms to stress both the message he preached and the manner in which he preached it.[294] λόγος and κήρυγμα therefore probably refer to the content and form of Paul's actual delivery.[295]

The idea of using ἀποδειξεις "manifestation" suggested the latter thought of proof.[296] The referring to "proof" needs to be taken properly. The Greek literally reads "of the Spirit and power" (του

[289] Taylor, *1 Corinthians*, 81.

[290] Fee, *The First Epistles to the Corinthians*, 92.

[291] Leon Morris, *The First Epistle of Paul to the Corinthians: An Introduction and Commentary* (Leicester: Inter-Varsity Press, 1958), 52.

[292] Hans Conzelmann, *A commentary on First Epistle to the Corinthians* (Philadelphia: Fortress Press, 1975), 54.

[293] Archibald Robertson and Alfred Plummer, *A Critical and Exegetical Commentary on the First Epistle of St. Paul to the Corinthians* (Edinburgh: T & T Clark, 1911), 32.

[294] Morris, *The First Epistle of Paul to the Corinthians*, 52.

[295] Fee, *The First Epistles to the Corinthians*, 94.

[296] C. K. Barrett, *A Commentary on the First Epistle to the Corinthians* (London: Adam & Charles Black, 1976), 65.

πνεύματος καί δυνάμεως) which refer to two realities, "spiritual gifts and miracles." But Paul used it interchangeably to speak of the Spirit is automatically to speak of power.[297]

4.3.5.2. Wisdom from Above Versus the Rulers of this Ages (vv. 6-7)

Birger Albert Pearson suggests that the opponents in Corinth had claimed to be τελείοι, and the context of the passage shows that they made this claim on the basis of their σοφία. There were undoubtedly some in Corinth who claimed to be a member of the spiritual elite οἱ τελείοι, over against those who had not yet arrived, the νήπιοι.[298]

4.3.5.2.1. τελείοις

The meaning of τελείος is commonly used by Philo from its secular usage in stoicism to denote one who has achieved the highest religious attainment, including "wisdom."[299] In the philosophical tradition, the word τελείοιi is used to refer to "the man of perfect wisdom."[300] The use of ἐν τοῖi τελείοις probably refers to the believers or saints.[301] According to Jerome Murphy-O Connor, some witnesses insert the adjective "human" before wisdom in order to underline that this term has a pejorative connotation here.[302]

---

[297] Fee, *The First Epistles to the Corinthians*, 95.

[298] Birger Albert Pearson, *The Pneumatikos–Psychikos Terminology in 1 Corinthians* (Missoula, Montana: Scholars Press, 1973), 28.

[299] Pearson, *The Pneumatikos–Psychikos Terminology in 1 Corinthians*, 28.

[300] Conzelmann, *A commentary on First Epistle to the Corinthians*, 60.

[301] Conzelmann, *A commentary on First Epistle to the Corinthians*, 60. H. Hubner suggests that in 1 Cor. 2:6 Paul addresses Christians as mature or a high class of believer to whom he may presume to offer the proclamation of his wisdom. See H. Hubner, "τελείοι," *EDNT* 3:343.

[302] Jerome Murphy-O Connor, The First Letter to the Corinthians," in *The New Jerome Biblical Commentary* (eds. Raymond E. Brown, Joseph A. Fitzmyer and Roland E. Murphy; Bangalore: Theological Publications in India, 1999), 801.

4.3.5.2.2. σοφία

The word σοφία occurs sixteen times in 1 Corinthians 1-3,[303] once in 1 Corinthians 12:8 and once in 2 Corinthians 1:12. Now it may be that in 2:6f, Paul is merely denying that the divine wisdom belongs to this age or its rulers, without asserting that they have a wisdom of their own.[304] In 1 Corinthians 2:2-16, he himself adopts the vocabulary and ideas of his opponents and is not afraid of the danger of using them in positive forms as this is possible in the light of the preceding antithesis in 1:18-2:5. This wisdom is described in 2:7 as a blessing of salvation wholly along the lines of the Jewish apocalyptic.[305] Paul's adversaries are Gnostics, but not Greek philosophers as the Corinthian gnosis was nourished by Hellenized Jewish apocalyptic speculation. Whenever Paul is speaking of lovgo" he is thinking not of traditional Greek rhetoric but of gnostic charismatic speech as the new wise men in Corinth probably want to impart a σοφία originating with cosmic-pneumatic powers.[306] It could be seen in Paul's argument in 2 Corinthians where he presented the gospel not as a rhetorical method, but as a Gnostic pneuma-christology.[307] When he presented the gospel, Paul reminds the Corinthians that the message which he preached to them was the uniform gospel preached by all the apostles.

4.3.5.2.3. ἣν προώρισεν[308]

Paul emphasizes that the "present" unveiling is indicated by the expression of εἰi δόξαν ἡμῶν "with a view to our glory," and δόξα describes our new being as supernatural.[309] This is the clause that clarifies both the content of "wisdom" and the identity of the

303 H. Hegermann, "σοφία," *EDNT* 3:258.

304 Barrett, *Essays on Paul*, 9.

305 Wilckens, "σοφία," *TDNT* 7:519.

306 H. Hegermann, "σοφία," *EDNT* 3:258.

307 Barrett, *Essays on Paul*, 7.

308 3rd person, singlular, aorist indicative active of προοριζω "to predetermine, foreordain, predestine."

309 *Conzelmann, A commentary on First Epistle to the Corinthians*, 62.

"mature" in verse 6.[310] Barrett argues that from the beginning, it was God's purpose to redeem mankind through Christ, and paradoxically self- giving wisdom was the mark of his purpose.[311] Thus, the divine predestination aims at the concrete historical revelation of what was previously hidden and is thus spoken of by Paul in a statement regarding salvation.[312]

4.3.5.3. The Rulers of this Age (v. 8)

The ἀρχοΰτων "rulers" which Paul mentioned in v. 6, 8 are probably not supernatural forces but earthly rulers who live according to the conventional wisdom of this world. They were believed to have access to the greatest amount of wisdom through God and their many counselors. Thus Paul's use of referring to ἀρχόντων "rulers" is to be understood as ironic because he was possibly thinking of emperors who had great love for rhetoric and philosophy.[313] Morris expresses that τῶν ἀρχόντων τοῦ αιῶνοi "the rulers of this world' is used to express demons by many scholars in both the ancient and moderns times.[314] O. Merk also suggested that ἀρχόντες in 1 Corinthians 2:6,8 refers not to earthly rulers, but to demonic powers.[315] Therefore, the question whether '*governing powers*' are demons or political powers has long been in dispute.[316] However, the

---

[310] Fee, *The First Epistles to the Corinthians*, 105.

[311] Barrett, *A Commentary on The First Epistle to the Corinthians*, 71.

[312] W. Radl, "προοριζω," *EDNT* 3:159.

[313] Witherington III, *Conflict & Community in Corinth*, 127.

[314] There is controversy on whether the text really mean forces of the unseen world. It should be noted that throughout this passage Paul's contrast is between the wisdom and the power of men. To introduce the thought of the wisdom of demonic powers is to bring in an extraneous concept. Moreover, attention should be given to v.8 where mention is made that the prince of this world were responsible for crucifying Christ in ignorance. Morris, *The First Epistle of Paul to the Corinthians,* 54.

[315] O. Merk, "ἄρχων," *EDNT* 2:168.

[316] Conzelmann, *A commentary on First Epistle to the Corinthians*, 61. Some scholars suppose that they are the earthly rulers who were responsible for the crucifixion. This view is possibly supported by verse 8 but much less likely in verse 6. See also Barrett, "The First Epistle to the Corinthians," 72.

most probable understanding of this is Jewish and Roman leaders.[317] Margareth E. Thrall suggested that Paul is simply referring to the ordinary human political authorities of his day that is the Roman Emperor and the various subordinate princes and magistrates who administer the province of the empire on his behalf.[318]

Fee comments on this passage saying that Paul elaborates the negative side of verse 6 but in light of the preceding description of God's wisdom. The reason for their misunderstanding is that it was "hidden in God" and could only be grasped by the revelation of God. He further mentions that what they did not understand was the nature of the true wisdom which stands in contradiction to human understanding.[319] Barrett expresses the misunderstanding of the earthly rulers on the basis that God's plan for salvation of the world is out of their wisdom and that they were in a state of ignorance about God's salvation.[320] The ignorance of the people was shadowed in the Old Testament where the prophet Isaiah speaks of that glorious event (Isa 64:3-4) and for the rulers of the nations who did not comprehend God's miraculous dealing with his people (Exo 5:2).[321] Witherington III also argues that the rulers of this world and their wisdom are in the process of passing away because the life, death and resurrection of Christ have transformed life's timeline. The things of the end time have broken into human history and have revitalized all purely human values, wisdom and structure.[322]

---

[317] Morris, *The First Epistle of Paul to the Corinthians*, 54. Some suppose that they are the earthly rulers who were responsible for the crucifixion of Jesus Christ. But this view is doubtful though possibilities could be seen in verse 8, but much less likely in verse 6 as the gospels represent the ministry, but not the death, of Jesus as a record of conflict with supernatural powers. See Barrett, "The First Epistle to the Corinthians," 72.

[318] Thrall, *The First and Second Letters of Paul to the Corinthians*, 25.

[319] Fee, *The First Epistles to the Corinthians*, 106.

[320] Barrett, "The First Epistle to the Corinthians," 72.

[321] Spurgeon,"1 Corinthians," 29.

[322] Witherington III, *Conflict & Community in Corinth*, 127.

4.3.5.4. Words Which the Spirit Teaches (vv. 9-13)

Although τῶν ἀρχόντων τοῦ αἰῶνος "the rulers of this world" could not understand the salvation plan of God, God revealed His wisdom to believers through the work of the Holy Spirit. The Holy Spirit was the one who makes known the mystery to Paul and the Corinthians because he has searched everything, even the deep things of God.[323] Barrett asserts that some commentators often show embarrassment in dealing with the relation between the Spirit of God, and with the reason for the Spirit's search or inquiry. He proposes that Paul is taking over the language of the Stoics in a different sense. The stoics supposed that they could by searching find God, and plumb the depths of His being. But for Paul, there is no profounder truth than the word of the cross, and only the Spirit can of Himself know, and then communicate the truth about God.[324]

4.3.5.5. A Natural Man Does Not Accept the Things of the Spirit of God (v. 14)

The reference to πνεύματος "spiritual" is an adjective derived from the noun "spirit", "πνεύμας whereas people who put their trust in this world are called ψυχικόι in contrast to those who trust the Spirit, who are called πνευματικόι.[325] According to A. Sand, Paul using ψυχικός refers to the "natural person" the human being with an earthly-worldly body which is shown like all else as perishable dishonorable, and weak.[326] The natural man is mostly defined negatively because he is a man who has not received the Holy Spirit.[327] Fee describes ψυχικόι in three terms, each in terms of their relationship, or lack thereof, to the Spirit. Firstly, these people do not have a relationship with God because they do not accept the things that come from God. Secondly, since their view is from the bottom, twisted and distorted, they were perishing in their judgment.

---

[323] Spurgeon, "1 Corinthians," 34.

[324] Barrett, "The First Epistle to the Corinthians," 74.

[325] Fee, *The First Epistles to the Corinthians*, 116.

[326] A Sand, "ψυχικός," *EDNT* 3:503.

[327] Barrett, "The First Epistle to the Corinthians," 77.

Thirdly, their inability to accept the Spirit makes them ignorant in the understanding of God.[328]

4.3.5.6. The Mind of Christ (v.16)

Paul's word νους probably means the thoughts of Christ as they are revealed by the Spirit. In the Greek Bible the word νους is translated from the Hebrew word *ruah* "רוּצ" which ordinarily means πνευμα.[329] Therefore, νους "mind" is here synonymous with νους "Spirit"[330] and probably refers to God's hidden wisdom[331] through the Spirit of Jesus Christ who made the Corinthians spiritual people.[332]

4.3.6. Theological Implication

An exegetical study on the selected texts reveals Paul's exhortation to the Corinthian Christians that the Holy Spirit of God was the one who made known the mystery to Paul and it was the Holy Spirit who knowing the mystery of God, reveals it to the Corinthian believers. Paul's message was not human wisdom, but it was divine wisdom imparted by God. The main motive was that Paul urges the Corinthian Christians not to depend on spiritual leaders but rather focus on Christ because it was not the wisdom that guaranteed the acceptance of the message of the message of the Cross of Christ. He strongly holds that it was the work of the Holy Spirit that opened the Corinthian hearts (1 Cor 2:1-6).[333] The Corinthian Christians thought that human wisdom was necessary to understand the gospel. So also the same misconception comes from the rulers of this world. They think themselves that they were wiser and take pride in their wisdom resulting in the crucifixion.[334] The problem of the Corinthians is that some Christians are not spiritual or do not have the Spirit of the mind of Christ. They are acting like non-Christians,

---

[328] Fee, *The First Epistles to the Corinthians*, 117.

[329] Fee, *The First Epistles to the Corinthians,* 119-120.

[330] Conzelmann, *A commentary on First Epistle to the Corinthians*, 69.

[331] Taylor, "1 Corinthians," 96.

[332] A. Sand, "νους," *EDNT* 2: 479.

[333] Spurgeon,"1 Corinthians," 32.

[334] Spurgeon,"1 Corinthians," 36.

and Paul's basic response is to give up all those practices because their practice has not caught up with what they have accepted in principle. Their cultural assumptions have not been critically evaluated in the light of their Christian faith and of the presence of God in their lives.[335]

4.4. Christians and the Law Courts (1 Cor 6:1-11)

4.4.1. Translation[336]

> [1]*Dare any of you having a matter against the other, to be judged before the unjust, and not before the saints?* [2]*Do you not know the saints shall judge the world? And if you are judged by the world, you are unworthy to judge very little matters"* [3]*Do you not know that we will judge an angels? Not to speak of the things of this life?* [4]*Therfore, if you have disputes indeed of this life, appoint as judge even the one who is being despised in the church.* [5]*I say this for your shame. Thus there is no room among you for wise men, who will be able to discern dispute between your brothers.* [6]*But one brother is judged against his own brothers, and this in front of unbelievers.* [7]*Now, therefore, you already have lawsuits with you which have been failed with yourselves. Why do you not rather take wrong? Why do you not rather be deprived?* [8]*But you do wrong and deprive, and that too your brothers.* [9]*Do you know that the unrighteousness shall not inherit the Kingdom of God; Do not be led astray; neither fornicators, nor idolaters nor adulterers nor male prostitutes nor homosexuality,* [10]*nor thieves nor covetousness nor drunkards nor slanderers nor swindlers shall inherit the kingdom of God.* [11]*And these things some of you were. But you were washed, sanctified and you were justified in the name of the Lord Jesus Christ and by the Spirit of our God.*

4.4.2. Introduction

Chapter 6 of 1 Corinthians has been traditionally divided into two parts, the first on a case in a pagan court involving different between

[335] Witherington III, *Conflict & Community in Corinth*, 129.

[336] The translation is from the Researcher's own.

two Christians (vv. 1-11) and the second on another case of sexual immorality.[337] This exegetical study examines the social situations in the Corinthian Community that Paul sees as the problem of lawsuits on two levels. The former looks to the community's relationship to the outside world. The latter looks at the community's internal life, where Paul understands the litigious nature of some Christians to be part of the larger problem of social division in the Corinthian churches.[338] Thus, this section raises the question of community borders, or what is appropriate within the community and of how the community relates to what is going on in the world outside the church.[339]

4.4.3. The Background

The Greco-Roman culture in which Paul and his converts lived offered a plethora of organizations, associations, and ways of making commitments. The secular world offered the raw material of the community and commitment out of which Paul creatively fashioned his understanding of the way Christians should live and comprehend their obligations to one another and to the world.[340] Before entering into the exegetical analysis, it is fitting to highlight some basic characteristics of the judicial process in a Roman colony. With the exception to the trial of Jesus, it appears that by the mid-first century CE, trial by jury was reserved mainly for criminal proceedings. Trial would be handled by some sort of judge and one of the earliest and most famous of Roman courts was the "extortion court."[341]

---

[337] Witherington III, *Conflict & Community in Corinth*, 164.

[338] Alan C. Mitchell, "Rich and Poor in the Courts of Corinth: Litigiousness and Status in 1 Corinthians 6:1-11," *NTS* 39 (1993): 562-586.

[339] Sampley, "The First Letter to the Corinthians," 855.

[340] J. Paul Sampley, *Pauline Partnership in Christ: Christian Community and Commitment in Light of Roman Law* (Philadelphia: Fortress Press, 1980), x.

[341] There was a three-stage judicial process for civil case in the Greco – Roman society. Firstly, the complainant would appear before one of the city's magistrate requesting a suit. If the magistrate agreed that there were grounds for a suit the defendant would be summoned by the plaintiff to court. The factual details of the case would be discussed and debated and a formula arrived at the final part. The trial would be based on what was in

Understanding the system of law courts in the Greco-Roman world helps one better understand the texts. If this is taken into 1 Corinthians 6, it appears that at the very least, one or both Christians going to court were probably well-to-do and hoped to exploit the judicial system to their advantage. Chapter 6 has been traditionally divided into two parts, the first part consists of a case in a pagan court involving differences between two Christians (vv. 1-11), and the second consists of another case of sexual immorality (vv. 12-22). Both cases discussed in chapter 6 deal with a serious breach of community and the ensuing bad Christian witnessed to the world.[342]

4.4.4. The Context

The critical issues addressed in 1 Corinthians 6:1-11 is communal.[343] According to Bruce W. Winter,[344] there are six issues which clarify Paul's discussion in 1 Corinthians 6:1-11: (i) the nature of civil litigation in Roman Corinth, (ii) Judges and οἱ ἄδικοι (iii) the powerful and οἱ ἄδικοι (iv) enmity and civil litigation (v) the arbiter and litigation and (vi) those least esteemed ἐν τῃ ἐκκλεσίᾳ. 1 Corinthians 6:1-11 addresses Paul's rhetorical questions initially to the man who was taking a brother to civil court in 6:2, but quickly turns to the whole assembly, which itself should be dealing with internal disputes in 6:3-6. In v. 7-8, Paul again addresses the disputants and continues his declaration in v. 9-11.[345] It should be noted that the intrusion of the vice lists in 6:9ff, with its explicit mention of sexual irregularities may lead us to connect verses 9-11 with the discussion of sexual immorality and purity following in

---

the formula. Secondly, the magistrate would then assign a judge, agreeable to both parties, to the case and pass along to him the formula. Finally, the case would be heard by the judge and the sentence passed, but it was the complainant's responsibility to see that the judgment was carried out by the defendant. Witherington III, *Conflict & Community in Corinth,* 162.

[342] See Witherington III, *Conflict & Community in Corinth,* 162.

[343] Mitchell, "Rich and Poor in the Courts of Corinth," 563.

[344] Bruce W. Winter, "Civil Litigation in Secular Corinth and the Church," *NTS* 37 (1991): 560.

[345] Horsley, *1 Corinthians,* 84.

6:12ff. On the other hand, one might assume that 6:9-11 is part of a loosely connected tradition added by Paul almost as afterthought.[346]

4.4.5. Exegetical Study of the Text

4.4.5.1. Taking Court Against the Unbelievers (v. 1)

F. F. Bruce comments that Paul was shocked to hear the news that some Corinthian Christians were persecuting others.[347] Even though the term ἀδικια refers to "wrongdoing,"[348] and this term is used here as 'unjustified' or 'unbelievers.'[349] Horsley's observations on this passage shows those who run the civil courts are unjust in their judgment. This is due to the reason that unrighteousness violates the divine principle of justice.[350] During the Greco-Roman times, the law and courts in the Roman Empire were forms of social controls, catering to the vested interests of the wealthy and powerful. Moreover, courts in the provinces gave preferential treatment to people of higher status and usually worked to the disadvantage of those of lower status.[351] Likewise, civil litigation in Roman Corinth, the right to prosecute was not granted to everyone. If the defendant was a parent, a patron, a magistrate, or a person of high rank, charges could not be brought by children, freedmen, private citizens, and men of low rank respectively. It was the practice that lawsuits were conducted between social equals who were from the powerful "οἱ δυνατοί" of the city, or by a plaintiff of superior social status and

---

[346] Lloyd A. Lewis, "The Law Courts in Corinth: An Experiment in the Power of Baptism," *ATR* 11 (1990): 89.

[347] Bruce, *1 and 2 Corinthians*, 59.

[348] "ἀδικια" *BAGD* 1:17.

[349] Bruce, *1 and 2 Corinthians*, 59.

[350] Horsley, *1 Corinthians*, 84. Dio Chrysostom, commenting on Roman Corinth about 100 CE says that there were "lawyers innumerable perverting justice" there and refers to young men declaiming forensic pieces in the courtyard next to the Temple of Poseidon during the Isthmian games, hoping to drum up business. Thus, K. Wengst has stressed that in view of the experiences listed in his tribulation catalogs (1 Cor 4:9ff; 2 Cor 11:23ff), Paul had little reason to trust Roman justice and that this passage should be read in that light. See Witherington III, *Conflict & Community in Corinth*, 164-165.

[351] Horsley, *1 Corinthians*, 84.

power against an inferior.[352] Paul's use of ἄδικοι refers to those who break God's laws, and therefore it comes to mean 'ungodly' or 'unrighteous.' The unrighteous who in contrast to the saints will not inherit the kingdom of God and they will be judged by the saints at the great eschatological judgment.[353] In such a context, the Gentiles are described in this way as despisers of the divine law that they cannot be expected to do justice.[354]

4.4.5.2. The Saints Will Judge the World (v. 2)

The idea of this judgment is based on Daniel 7:22 in the sense that judgment was given to the saint of the Most High. These saints are the associates of the Son of Man, the appointed judges of the living and the dead.[355] Paul's Jewish apocalyptic worldview holds that those saints as the citizens of the eschatological society will judge the present world.[356] It was observed that the Corinthians' problems arose not just from bad ethics or bad social values, but from bad theology which affected all worldly affairs and matters including sexual and legal matters. They had an inadequate knowledge of the future eschatology that was shaping their values and decision making.[357]

4.4.5.2.1. κριτηρίων ἐλαξίστων

It is suggested that the action initiated by Christians against their fellow believers came within the scope of vexatious litigation. In Roman circles, litigation could came with personal enmity and was used to aggravate personal enmity. The same problem was brought into the Corinthian church because of personal loyalty to Christian teachers in the church. This issue of Christian leadership was also expressed in litigation, with one of the leading Christians taking

---

352 Winter, *After Paul Left Corinth*, 60.

353 Fee, *The First Epistles to the Corinthians*, 232.

354 Schrenk, "αδικος", *TDNT* 1:151.

355 Dan 7:13.cf. Matt 16:27; Jn 5:27; Acts 17:31. see Bruce, *1 and 2 Corinthians,* 60.

356 Horsley, *1 Corinthians,* 84-85.

357 See Witherington III, *Conflict & Community in Corinth*, 16.

another to court.[358] The argument which forbids them from taking cases of internal conflict to civic courts make it abundantly clear that Paul thought of his assemblies as local communities of an effective community that would take care of its own affairs without interacting at all with the official political orders.[359]

4.4.5.3. We Are to Judge Angels (v. 3)

In the last days, human beings as well as angels will appear in God's court. Fee suggested that the question οὐκ οἴδατε ὅτι ἀγγελους κρινοῦμεν, μήτιγε βιωτικά probably reflects an apocalyptic motif as to the judgment of fallen angels.[360] Bruce also commented that it could refer to the disobedient angels who are held in the eternal chains in deepest darkness until the judgment of the great day (cf. Jude 6).[361]

4.4.5.4. Appointing Judges from the Community (v. 4)

There is a dilemma about the main verse in 6:4 whether it is indicative or imperative since the second person plural form, καθίζετε which occurs in end of the sentence can be either indicative or imperative.[362] Bruce Winter suggests the NIV translation as imperative which is preferred here: "Therefore, if you have disputes about such matters, appoint as judges even men of little account in the church". This shows that while secular judges were people of high status in the community, in the Christian gathering secular status had no place.[363] The phrase τους ἐξουθηένημέους ἐν τῇ ἐκκλησία would be that the least esteemed among them are competent to settle their

---

[358] Winter, *After Paul Left Corinth*, 65.

[359] Richard A. Horsley, "The First and Second Letters to the Corinthians," in *A Postcolonial Commentary on the New Testament Writings* (eds. Fernando F. Segovia and R. S. Sugirtharajah; London: T & T Clark, 2007), 231.

[360] cf. 2 Pet 2:4; Jude 6:1. Fee, *The First Epistles to the Corinthians*, 234.

[361] Bruce, *1 and 2 Corinthians*, 59. Carl Schneider uses καθίζετε as figurative meaning for judges. See Carl Schneider, "καθηεμαι," *TDNT* 3:444.

[362] Taylor, "1 Corinthians," 146.

[363] Bruce Winter, *1 Corinthians* (NBC; Illinois: Inter-Varsity Press, 1994), 1169.

disputes.[364] The word ἐάν with the subjunctive carries a construction that such lawsuits should not arise.[365]

4.4.5.5. No One to Decide Dispute Between One Believer and Another (v. 5)

The language of 6:1-11 indicates that the offenders were among the wise and those of the higher status.[366] Here, the word σοφός is negatively used in the letter and its use in 6:5 fits that pattern. Theissen observes that the ironic question about whether anyone is σοφός enough to decide their own lawsuits points to these people as the offenders.[367] Even though Christians were capable of applying the resources of their secular education in disputes which could normally be settled by a civil action, they used it against others creating havoc and disunity within the church.[368] Moreover, the Corinthian Christians were boasting of their wisdom and knowledge,[369] but Paul is trying to help the Corinthians to see their true condition over against their perceived one. A trial between two brothers before pagan courts reveals how lacking in truly Christian wisdom they are, and therefore it shows how poorly they understand their true place in Jesus Christ.[370]

4.4.5.6. Believers Goes to Court Against Believers (v. 6)

The shameful practice is precisely described. The expression describes the fact that "brother goes against brother, and that before unbelievers". Here the word ἀδελφός meant more familial relationship than a physical sense as it denote "physical brotherhood"

---

[364] Taylor, "1 Corinthians," 146.

[365] Morris, *1 The First Epistle of Paul to the Corinthians*, 94.

[366] Wilckens, "σοφία," *TDNT* 7:517.

[367] During Paul's period, the secular education consisted not only of intensive instruction in literature but also of training in oratory including forensic skills. They engaged in declamation pieces before their fellow pupils and were also taught to evaluate court cases. See Mitchell, "Rich and Poor in the Courts of Corinth," 572.

[368] Winter, "Civil Litigation in Secular Corinth and the Church," 569.

[369] Lewis, "The Law Courts in Corinth," 92.

[370] Fee, *The First Epistles to the Corinthians*, 236.

in the strict sense or more generally the "spiritual brotherhood" of Israelites or Christians.[371] The word had become part of Christian expression, borrowed from the vocabulary of Israel, which indicates membership in the church.[372] Thus in v.6, Paul states that it is scandalous for members of the church to place their cases before pagan judges. By virtue of their participation in the final judgment of the world, the members of the church will stand as judge over pagan judges.[373]

4.4.5.7. You Have Been Defeated Completely (v. 7)

It is true that private arbitration[374] provided Paul with an attractive solution to the problem. Ben Witherington III asserts that Paul's expression of going to pagan court has amount to moral failure[375] whatever the result of the legal process.[376] In v. 8, Paul introduces a condemnation of litigation among Christians. The adverb ὅλος translated "completely" is the same adverb translated "actually" in 5:1.[377] The preferable way would be to bear wrong and defraud. Thus, a member of the church would suffer injustice, rather than to

---

[371] Von Soden, "ἀδελφός," *TDNT* 1:144.

[372] When Christian communities uses this figurative language, it is certainly following what had been done by Judaism. "άδελφός" in Septuagint means "brother Jew" and άδελφός becomes thus the term for Christians. This linguistic customs was so noticeable that the pagan made scornful remarks about it. See Lewis, "The Law Courts in Corinth," 92.

[373] Lewis, "The Law Courts in Corinth," 95.

[374] In private arbitration, two parties mutually agreed upon a third person, who would settle a difference between them. This extra-judicial procedure in Greco-Roman society could be quite effective because of the advantages it had over other methods of litigation. Its advantages are: (i) There was no need for Roman official involvement in legal matters, so it could be conducted on a strictly in-house basis. (ii) Since it did not involve in the establishment of a separate court or tribunal it did not require a special privilege from the Imperial administration. (iii) Because any third party could be selected as an arbiter, there was no need for a system of special judges.(iv) It was less costly than going to court. See Mitchell, "Rich and Poor in the Courts of Corinth," 568.

[375] Witherington III, *Conflict & Community in Corinth*, 166.

[376] Morris, *1 The First Epistle of Paul to the Corinthians*, 96.

[377] Taylor, "1 Corinthians," 147.

pursue the suit.[378] The implication of the warning that follows is that such a practice is not only shameful but simply cannot be tolerated in the Christian community.[379]

4.4.5.8. You Yourselves are Wrong and Defraud (v. 8)

The Corinthian Christians were not only denying suffering for the sake of Christ, but also in making these accusations were actively doing wrong to others. Those in Christ should have a special care for one another. But the Corinthian Christians were sinning against ethical standards, and they were sinning against loving one another in brotherly love.[380] The expression ἀδικεῖτε καί ἀποστερεῖτε does not mean that they have become criminals in the legal sense.[381] What Paul says is that even when they are wrong, they wronged others by taking them to the court. It is thus far better to suffer wrong, to be cheated, than to detract from the reputation of the gospel before the unbelieving world and to wrong other believers.[382]

4.4.5.9. Unjust Will Not Inherit the Kingdom of God (vv. 9, 10)

Paul rarely refers to the kingdom of God in his letter and altogether there are four places that he refers to the kingdom of God viz. 6:9, 10; 15: 50 and Galatians 5. 21.[383] Verses 9, 10 lists those who will not inherit the kingdom of God. Those are πόρνει "fornicators," εἰδωλολάτραι "idolaters." μοιχοί "adulterers," μαλακοί "male prostitutes," ἀρσενοκοῖται "homosexuality," κλεπται "thieves," πλεονέκται "covetous persons," μέθυσοι "drunkards," λοίποδοι "revilers," and ἅρπαγες "rapacious persons." Amongst those listed the term μαλακοί and ἀρσενοκοῖται are heavily debated.[384] Dionysius of Halicurnassus uses this term to refer to a young male

[378] Lewis, "The Law Courts in Corinth," 95.

[379] Fee, *The First Epistles to the Corinthians*, 243.

[380] Morris, *1 The First Epistle of Paul to the Corinthians*, 96.

[381] Conzelmann, *A commentary on First Epistle to the Corinthians*, 106.

[382] Taylor, "1 Corinthians," 148.

[383] Barrett, "The First Epistle to the Corinthians," 77.

[384] Witherington III, *Conflict & Community in Corinth*, 166.

prostitute as the molestation of minors by an adult male which was the most common form of sexuality in antiquity. Therefore both μαλακοί and ἀρσενοκοῖται respectively refers to the leading and following partners in homosexual activities.[385] Paul reminds the Corinthians of what they used to be in contrast to what they now are by virtue of their conversion.[386]

4.4.5.10. You Were Washed, Sanctified and Justified (v. 11)

The Corinthian Christians' history was polluted with various offences which lead them to immorality. But those inhuman practices were washed away by the suffering and death of Jesus Christ. These metaphors of salvation declared them "washed" from the degradation of their former practices, "set apart" for ethical life according to God's will, and "justified."[387] The idea of salvation, which is formulated in terms of a Jewish apocalyptic worldview perceives atonement not only for individual offences, but also in terms of bringing about an entirely new order where the conditions that give rise to societal and structural sin would be eradicated.[388] The past tense of all these verbs indicates that Paul is referring to a definite event in the past, namely the conversion of the Christians he is addressing.[389]

4.4.6. Theological Implication

The problem addressed in 1 Corinthians 6:1-11 has been described in light of Paul's expectations for their relationship with the outside world in the practical matter of settling disputes. Within the Corinthian society, one Christian ought to treat another regardless of their social status in society, but they revert to their pre-conversion state which tends to lead to betrayal of their baptism, when they act like ἄδικοι and ἄπιστοι.[390] According to Horsley, the passages reflected somehow the recognized implication of the separation of

---

[385] Witherington III, *Conflict & Community in Corinth*, 166.

[386] Taylor, "1 Corinthians," 148.

[387] Horsley, *1 Corinthians,* 87.

[388] Crocker, *Reading 1 Corinthians in the Twenty-First Century*, 71.

[389] Witherington III, *Conflict & Community in Corinth*, 167.

[390] Mitchell, "Rich and Poor in the Courts of Corinth," 569.

religion and politics. Here, the apocalyptic orientation of Paul's mission was rooted in the experience of a subject people dominated by the Seleucid and Roman imperial regimes. The main intention of Jewish apocalyptic literature was to enhance the resolve of the Jewish communities to persist in their traditional way of life and maintain their independence of the dominant imperial society. In such a context, Paul's understanding of the dominant order and its people as practitioners of injustice. By contrast, the communities he was establishing were supposedly communities of justice separated from the world.[391]

4.4.7. Conclusion

From the above exegetical studies, it can be assumed that Paul in Romans 13:1-7 deals with aspects of the role of the rulers, including jurisdiction over criminal cases. Paul discusses the attitude of the Christian citizen and his obedience to the law. It includes a recognition of the right to administer criminal law which arose from the divine *imperium* held by Government. In 1 Corinthians chapter 2 and 6, Paul discusses both the faith of the Christians not to rely on their faith in spiritual leaders but to depend on Christ Jesus. He further discusses the nature of civil litigation in Corinth with Christians taking fellow Christians to court on small issues.[392] Civil litigation came within the purview of local honorary magistrates who appointed judges or juries comprised of the well-to-do in that city known for their partiality.[393] As a whole, we can suggested that Paul may have been influenced in his ethical teaching by Greco-Roman ethical codes and by the Old Testament. Nevertheless, he sees everything through the lens of Jesus Christ which would be the best fit for the living standards of Christians in his own time.

---

[391] Horsley, *1 Corinthians,* 88.

[392] Winter, "Civil Litigation in Secular Corinth and the Church," 560.

[393] Winter, "Civil Litigation in Secular Corinth and the Church," 57.

Chapter 5

Implications for Religion and Politics in Mizoram with Reference to Church and State Relations in Pauline Epistles

5.1. Introduction

The preceding chapter deals with the Pauline understanding and teaching of how Christians should be involved in the social and political life in the first century CE. The main emphasis is that all authorities and rulers were undoubtedly ordained by God. But at the same time, there is a reason that Christians should be cautious with regard to the relationship between religion and politics. While drawing the implications of the relationship between the church and the State in Pauline Epistles for Mizoram, the understanding of the relationship between religion and politics in Mizoram which is presently in a state of confusion. Many Mizos are in a dilemma on this issue because some have upheld an ideology of separating the church from politics. But at the same time, many people think that the church should raise her voice as it is the teaching of the Bible and mandatory for the well-being of the people. Thus, this chapter tries to bring out the history and identity of the Mizos before and after Christianity in Mizoram and an attempt will be made to apply what Paul has in view of the relationship between church and State in his epistles to the Mizo context. Moreover, what has been considered relevant from the previous chapters will be taken up for further discussion in this chapter.

5.2. Socio-Political History of Pre-Christian Mizos

Mizoram lies in the eastern corner of India and is bordered on the north by Assam and Manipur, on the west by Tripura and the Chittagong Hill tracts of Bangladesh, and on the east and south by the Chin state of Myanmar. It has an area of 21,090 sq. kilometers and is lying between 20.20^0 E and 93.29^0 E longitude. The Tropic of Cancer runs through the heart of Mizoram which is crossing the village of Thenzawl.[394] Mizos were formerly known as "Lushai"[395] and came to be known as "Mizo"[396] only in the year 1954 when the name "Lushai Hills" was changed to "Mizo Hills" by an Act of Parliament.[397] The present name "Mizoram" has been used only from 1972. It had diverse culture and traditions in the beginning, but the coming of Christianity has united the people culturally, socially and politically.

5.2.1. The Lal (Chief)

A village-system of government was followed under the local chief known as *"The Lal"*[398] before the British took over administration

---

[394] Mangkhosat Kipgen, *Christianity and Mizo Culture* (Aizawl, Mizoram: Mizo Theological Conference, 1997), 30.

[395] Various derivations are suggested for the word "Lushai." Some of the common interpretations are *Lu* as head, *sha as* cut and some others as *Lu* means head, *shei* means Long. See Sangkima, *Mizos: Society and Social Change: 1890-1047* (Delhi: Spectrum Publications, 1992), 8.

[396] The term means *Mi*= man and *Zo*– a cold place at a high altitude. See *Sangkima, Mizos: Society and Social Change*, 9.

[397] Lalchungnunga, *Mizoram: Politics of Regionalism and National Integration* (New Delhi: Reliance Publishing House,1994), 26.

[398] Vanlalchhuanawma, *Christianity and Subaltern Culture: Revival Movement as a Cultural Response to Westernisation in Mizoram* (Delhi: ISPCK, 2006), 28.

of Mizoram. Every village had its own chief and was a sovereign independent state under its chief.[399] The people considered the chief as the supreme authority of the village and everything was subject to his leadership.[400] Though there were many different clan chiefs in the early Mizos, the chiefs administration were generally similar in pattern. The chief house was mostly situated at the centre of the village and it had a huge flat place in front, called the "chief palace."[401]

All the chiefs were bound by traditional laws.[402] The chiefs were the ultimate decision makers for their respective villages and all cases were brought to him for trial.[403] Since the chiefs were honored and respected, it was his duty to protect the life and property of the villages and administer justice according to the traditional laws.[404] Whenever the people were distressed and in need of help, the village chief would help them. The villagers in return would render their complete support the chief.[405] According to Lalchungnunga, the chief enjoyed the following privileges, such as, six tinful of paddy from every household out of the annual harvest, the left fore-leg of any animal killed, one-tenth of the amount of salt collected from the village, a share of any wild honey collected by the villagers, a share of fish caught in any fishing expedition and free labour in constructing his house.[406]

---

[399] Chhangte Lal hminga, *The Life and Witness of the Church in Mizoram* (Serkawn: The Literature Committee of the Baptist Church of Mizoram, 1987), 6.

[400] H. Lalrinthanga, *Church and State Relationship in the Mizo Socio-Political Life: 1952-2006* (Delhi: ISPCK, 2013), 12.

[401] B. Lalthangliana, *India, Burma & Bangladesh Mizo Chanchin* (Aizawl: Remkungi, 2001), 283.

[402] Lalchungnunga, *Mizoram: Politics of Regionalism and National Integration*, 28.

[403] V. L. Siama, *Mizo History* (Aizawl: Lalrinliana, 1953), 17.

[404] Lalchungnunga, *Mizoram: Politics of Regionalism and National Integration*, 28.

[405] N. E. Parry, *A Monograph on Lushai Customs and Ceremonies* (Assam: Assam Government Press, 1976), 19.

[406] Lalchungnunga, *Mizoram: Politics of Regionalism and National Integration*, 30.

5.2.2. The Upa (The Council of Elders)

The council of elders known as *Upa* was appointed by the chief to assist him in the administration of the village.[407] The chief was expected to appoint whoever he deemed fit for the post, but usually they were chosen from among the *Thangchhuahs,*[408] who were regarded as reputed public figures and representatives of the different clans found in the village. Although all powers is theoretically in their hands, the village chiefs will never try a case without consulting their elders and as a rule three or four elders tried cases along with the chief.[409] The involvement of elders in the decision making process in administration provided a broader representation of the people's interests.[410] The chiefs and council of elders normally faced no opposition in their decisions as fairness could be seen in their judgment.[411]

5.2.3. Village Officials

Besides the council of elders, there were other village officials. The *Tlangau* (village Crier),[412] the *Thirdeng* (Village Blacksmith),[413] the *Puithiam* (Priest),[414] the *Ramhuals* (Advisors concerning land to be

---

[407] Kipgen, *Christianity and Mizo Culture*, 59.

[408] *Thangchhuah* title was considered honorific title among the villagers and also have the right of admission to heavenly place after death. J. Besides, *Thangchhuah Pa* should also give public feast at least four times culminating giving away the treasures in their possession. Shakespear, *The Lushei Kuki Clans* (London: Macmillan and Co., Ltd., 1912), 63-64.

[409] Bimal and Lahiri, *Lushai Customs and Ceremonies*, 1.

[410] Kipgen, *Christianity and Mizo Culture*, 59.

[411] Kipgen, *Christianity and Mizo Culture*, 59.

[412] The one who proclaimed the chief's order to the village.

[413] He has to repair the tools of the villagers and in turn, he gets a basket of rice from each house in the village after the harvest, as a rule.

[414] There were two types of *Puithiam*, the former one is the *Sadawt*, appointed by the chief to serve as the official priest for the entire village. The other, the *Bawlpu* was appointed by the clan group to serve its needs. Both of them served as healers and leaders of the village in all matters pertaining to religion, and receives their remuneration from the members of the community in proportion to their services.

cultivated),[415] and the *Khawchhiar* (Village Writers).[416] All these officials represented the social, religious, political and economic conditions of the early Mizo society.

5.2.4. Economic System

The system of paddy cultivation was the primitive means of livelihood and is the main basis of the economy of the Mizos. It appears that hunting and trapping did not much affect their economy but raids and inter-feuds disturbed the general life of the people which sometimes required guarding of people working in the jhum. Yet the people were content with their economy because they had limited wants.[417] Wealth was never sought after for its own sake, except as adventure and for some use. For them, there was no value of wealth apart from the joy of sharing with neighbours the good things they had.[418]

5.2.5. Social Life

The Mizos of the olden days were semi-nomadic tribes. The community was centred around their chief. The village therefore remained united as a family.[419] Each village was self-contained, self-governing and had to be self-sufficient. This autonomous village-system generally worked well and ensured the limited needs of its

---

The system of remuneration varies in different villages and is again a matter of local arrangement. Kipgen, *Christianity and Mizo Culture,* 60.

[415] They are the people who advise where jhums should be cultivated each year and are allowed first choice of fields to cultivate. Bimal and Lahiri, *Lushai Customs and Ceremonies,* 7.

[416] The village writers duty is to keep the village statistics registers, the village house, the roaster of people who are liable to be called on for labour work and a list of all guns in the village. Parry, *A Monograph on Lushai Customs and Ceremonies,* 7

[417] Sangkima, *Mizos: Society and Social Change,* 48.

[418] Lalsawma, *Revival: The Mizo Ways* (Aizawl, Mizoram: Lalsawma, 1994), 20.

[419] C. Pazawna, "Christianity in Mizoram: Vision for the Twenty-First Century," in *Ground Works for Tribal Theology in the Mizo Context* (RMCS 1; eds. Rosiamliana Tochhawng, K. Lalrinmawia & L. H. Rawsea; Delhi: ISPCK, 2007), 50-51. See also Malsawmdawngliana, *Negotiating the Past: Memory, History and Culture of Mizo* (Guwahati: Scientific Book Centre, 2015), 108-109.

primitive community were met.[420] This kind of traditional living gave them self-reliance. They fostered basic skills and simple virtues. Honesty, courage, self-discipline, mutual help, a readiness to organize and be organized were all highly prize and in fact were largely summed up in the untranslatable word *Tlawmngaihna*.[421] Under the guidance of the chief, they were neither rich nor poor in their living as each family lived on its own produce.[422] Thefts were almost unheard of and locks and keys were unknown.[423] Thus, it can be said assumed that Mizo society was a free, patriarchal and closely knit society with no class distinctions.[424]

5.3. Religious Beliefs

The primitive religion of the Mizos has been described as animism, which lexically means "attribution of soul to the inanimate objects or natural phenomena."[425] The following are some of the major beliefs of the Mizo religion.

---

[420] J. Meirion Lloyd, *History of the Church in Mizoram* (Aizawl, Mizoram: Synod Publication Board, 1991), 3.

[421] Tlawmngaihna is a Mizo term which literally means resistance to being helped by others by helping others who are in need. The emphasis is on a denial of self rather than an effort to be independent. Its purpose is to serve the community and any person in the community who are in need of help. It is an act of charity wherein self-interest is subordinated to the interest of the community, and the self sacrifices for the need of others is to come in spontaneously as a natural part of one's life. K. Thanzauva, *Theology of Community: Tribal Theology in the Making* (Aizawl, Mizoram: Mizo Theological Conference, 1997), 120.

[422] K. Zawla, *Mizo Pi Pute leh An Thlahte Chanchin* (Aizawl: Lalnipuii, 2011), 151.

[423] John Vanlal Hluna, *Church & Political Upheaval in Mizoram* (Aizawl, Mizoram: Mizo History Association, 1985), 8.

[424] K. Thanzauva, "Introduction," in *Toward a Tribal Theology: The Mizo Perspective* (ed. K. Thanzauva; Mizoram: Mizo Theological Conference, 1989), 4.

[425] Lalsawma, *Revival: The Mizo Ways*, 32.

5.3.1. Pathian

The Mizos believed in one supreme God called *Pathian*[426] who is their overlord.[427] As cited by C. L. Hminga, Rev. Liangkhaia[428] believed that the traditional Mizo religion had its origin in the consciousness of their needs for deliverance from illness and from other misfortunes which they attributed to evil spirits.[429] This god was perceived to be a male deity and a benevolent being, and was considered to be the creator and sustainer of all things.[430] Lalsawma asserts that god as *Pathian* was the Sovereign Absolute, the final court of Appeal, the ultimate dispenser of Justice.[431] It was to him men prayed when they were in troubled circumstances.[432] Hence, Pathian was conceived as the one who saw the people from above and was willing to help them and uphold justice.[433] It seems that the idea of a spirit other than *Pathian* seems to have prevailed in the pre-Christian era of the Mizos.[434]

---

[426] *Pa* means father and *thian* derives from the word *thiang* means holy. See Thanzauva, *Theology of Community*, 152.

[427] A. C. Ray, *Mizoram* (New Delhi: Ministry of Information and Broadcasting Corporation, 1972), 9.

[428] Born in the year 1884 and being one of the first Pastor among Mizo, Liangkhaia embraced by Christianity during the first Wave of Revival movement in Mizoram, he severely suffered persecution as persecution was at it height. He encountered beating, ill-treatments and many tortures that left him discomfort in his body all through his life. See Lalsawma, *Revival: The Mizo Ways,* 145.

[429] The believed in the existence of spirits are Phung, Khawhring, Hmuithla, Pheichham, Maimi, Rawt, Taumeichher Chhi, Chawm, Tual Hik, Dengsur, Sih Huai and Hautaii. Lal Biak Thanga, *The Mizos: A Study in Racial Personality* (Gauhati: United Publishers, 1978), 26.

[430] L. H. Lalpekhlua, *Contextual Christology: A Tribal Perspective* (Delhi: ISPCK, 2007), 180.

[431] Lalsawma, *Revival: The Mizo Ways*, 25.

[432] Zairema, "The Mizo and Their Religion," in *Toward a Tribal Theology: The Mizo Perspective* (ed. K. Thanzauva; Mizoram: Mizo Theological Conference, 1989), 38.

[433] Lalpekhlua, *Contextual Christology*, 182.

[434] Lalmuanawma Renthlei, "The Concept of 'King' and 'Kingdom' in John's Gospel: Implications for Religio-Politics Relationship in Mizo Context," (M. Th Diss., Senate of Serampore College, 2016), 64.

5.3.2. Sakhua

The Mizo word for religion is *Sakhua*. However, as the early concept of *Sakhua* was narrow and limited, it has been understood only superficially.[435] The etymology of *Sakhua* is unclear. Literally, *sa* means 'animal' and *khua* means 'village' or 'weather.'[436] But the religious connotation goes much deeper than that. Kipgen states that *sa* stands for the god worshipped by the ancestors and *khua* for nature or creation.[437] He further states that *Sa* was worshipped with an offering of a pig sacrifice, and *Khua* was worshipped with the sacrifice of a mithun.[438] Zairema believes that sakhua was the clan god, who built up, protected and cared for the family.[439] Undoubtedly, *sakhua* among the early Mizos refers to the relation of a family to its god and all the necessary rituals, performances and attitude associated with that.[440]

5.3.3. Life After Death

The early Mizos believed that humans were immortal. They believed that the spirits of the dead dwelt in two places. They were known as *Mitthi Khua* (The village of the dead) and *Pialral* (The land beyond the *Pial* river-Paradise).[441] *Mitthi Khua* was the abode of the departed souls of the commoners. It was believed to be a shadowy world where everything was on a much lower scale than in the present world.[442] They had to work hard to earn their living. Those who are poor in the world continue to remain poor and hard working. There was no rest

---

435 Vanlalchhuanawma, *Mission and Tribal Identity: A Historical Analysis of the Mizo Synod Mission Board from a Tribal Perspective: 1953-1981* (Delhi: ISPCK, 2010), 48.

436 Zairema, "The Mizo and their Religion," 35.

437 Kipgen, *Christianity and Mizo Culture*, 112.

438 Kipgen, *Christianity and Mizo Culture*, 112.

439 Zairema, "The Mizo and Their Religion," 35.

440 Vanlalchhuanawma, *Mission and Tribal Identity*, 48.

441 Pazawna, "Christianity in Mizoram," 50.

442 It was comparable to the Hebrew concept of Sheol. See Kipgen, *Christianity and Mizo Culture,* 118.

and pleasure.[443] On the far side of *Mitthi Khua*, was located *Pialral*, the abode of bliss. Access to *Pialral* was not obtained by virtue, but by performance of sacrifices, killing certain specified animals or a person who was a *Thangchhuah*.[444] It was the culmination of redemption or salvation in the traditional belief.[445]

5.3.4. Salvation

According to the traditional belief of the Mizos in Pre-Christian Era, three groups of people were privileged to enter full salvation. The first are the *Hlamzuihs*, the babies who die in infancy and are buried without ceremony under the house. The second was a young man who had sexual relations with either three virgin girls or seven women. The third and most important was that of *Thangchhuah*.[446] There were two kinds of *Thangchhuah*: (i) *Thangchhuah* at home (*In lama Thangchhuah*), and (ii) *Thangchhuah* in the Jungle (*Ram lama Thangchhuah*). The former required a person with genuine ambition and super wealth. It consisted of eight stages Each of these stages required a specific number of animals, alcohols and public feasts. In order to become *Thangchhuah* at home, the minimum requirements of animals were: nine male pigs, seven female pigs, twelve piglings, three fowls, seven mithun. The latter required a person to kill a number of specified animals such as elephant, bear, sambhur, barking deer, a wild boar, a full grown mithun, a poisonous snake called *Rulngan* and a species of eagle called *Muvanlai*.[447] All the Mizo men tried to attain *Thangchhuah* for the salvation of their spirit after

---

[443] Lalrinmawia, "Pialral Theology," 145.

[444] Vanlalchhuanawma, *Mission and Tribal Identity*, 48. Those spirits of *Thangchhuah* would go directly to *Pialral* where there is no more need of work. They would stay there forever enjoying all the good things. They enjoy life in its fullness there and lack nothing they wish because everything is provided there free of costs. See K. Lalrinmawia, "Pialral Theology: Mizo Expression of Theology," in *Ground Works for Tribal Theology in the Mizo Context* (RMCS 1; eds. Rosiamliana Tochhawng, K. Lalrinmawia & L. H. Rawsea; Delhi: ISPCK, 2007), 145.

[445] Lalrinmawia, "Pialral Theology," 145.

[446] Kipgen, *Christianity and Mizo Culture*, 121.

[447] Vanlalchhuanawma, *Mission and Tribal Identity*, 51.

death.[448] He will be served by persons whom he killed and this was the root cause of head hunting in the early Mizo history.

5.4. Religio-Political History of Post-Christian Mizos

5.4.1. Communalization of Religion

With the arrival of missionaries in Mizoram,[449] Christianity grew at an extraordinary pace in Mizoram. The missionaries emphasized Jesus Christ as a Saviour from the power of evils and called the Mizo people to accept him and discard their old religion.[450] The understanding of Christ as victor over spirits proved to be an effective instrument of evangelization in Mizo society.[451] The traditional Mizo concept of God was adopted by the pioneer Christian missionaries to represent the Christian God.[452] For those who accepted the message, it was no longer necessary to make attempts to earn entrance into *Pialral*. The religious meaning of head-hunting was removed which help them to adjust to the new political situation imposed by the British government.[453] Meanwhile, Christians were persecuted in various places and some of the methods employed were physical obstructions, pressed labour, fine, torture and expulsion from

---

448 Lalrinmawia, "Pialral Theology," 145.

449 The most significant history was marked by the visit of Rev. William Williams who set out on February 15, 1891 for Mizoram and arrived Aizawl on 20th March, 1891. He was the first who made an attempt to communicate to the Mizos about the Christian God. See Kipgen, *Christianity and Mizo Culture,* 191-197. However, there is another assumption of the arrival of Rev. William Williams as 15th March, 1891 and the latter in most accepted by the people. Lalhruaitluanga Ralte, *Zoram Vartian: Chanchintha leh Thuziak Khaw Var Tan Dan* (Aizawl: Fineprints, 2008), 168.

450 Lalpekhlua, *Contextual Christology*, 94.

451 Lalpekhlua, *Contextual Christology*, 95.

452 C. L. Hminga. "The Traditional Mizo Concept of God," in *Towards Tribal Theology: A Mizo Perspective* (ed. K. Thanzauva; Aizawl: Mizo Theological Conference, 1989), 51.

453 F, Hrangkhuma, "The Mizos: A People Transformed by the Gospel," in *Ground Works for Tribal Theology in the Mizo Context* (RMCS 1; eds. Rosiamliana Tochhawng, K. Lalrinmawia & L. H. Rawsea; Delhi: ISPCK, 2007), 10.

the villages.[454] Christianity was somehow looked upon as foreign, imported and inducted into society by foreigners so that it took more time to accept the new religion.

5.4.2. Political Upheavals in Mizo Society

After the annexation of Mizoram by the British, all political activity were strictly forbidden in Mizoram. The purpose of the British administration was not trade, but to keep peace with the Mizos. They therefore spend as little time and money as possible for administering the land and the people. It is often said that the British did not interfere much in the daily lives of the Mizos.[455] In spite of this, attempt had been made in the third decade of the 20th century by some Mizos to form a sort of political organization. But it was suppressed by the British because of the fear of uprising. But the Second World War changed that condition and the Government started seeking the support of the chiefs in their war effort. Hence, the formation of a political party was permitted by the Superintendent. Thus a new era dawned in the political history of the Mizos.[456] Under the sixth Schedule of the Constitution of India, the District Council was set up in 1952 where its responsibilities included establishment of village councils and town committees, marriage and social customs, levy on taxes professions, trades and employment.[457] Under the provisions of the Sixth Schedule of the Constitution of India, The Mizo District Council was inaugurated on the 25th April, 1952. The Party ultimately abolished a total number of 309 Mizo chieftainships by a Resolution in the Autonomous District Council and the Resolution to that effect was approved by the Legislative Assembly to be in force with effect from the 16th August, 1954.[458] But there was significant changes in the pattern of civil administration in the village after the

---

[454] Lalsawma, *Revival: The Mizo Ways*, 40-41.

[455] Hrangkhuma, "The Mizos: A People Transformed by the Gospel," 4.

[456] P. Lalnithanga, *Political Development in Mizoram* (Revised & Enlarged; Aizawl: P. Lalnithanga, 2006), 8.

[457] Ray, *Mizoram,* 16.

[458] Lalchungnunga, *Mizoram: Politics of Regionalism and National Integration*, 39.

disturbance of 1966, which led to the formation of Group centres and its consequent effects will be dealt with later.[459]

5.4.3. Social Changes

The coming of the gospel strongly shocked the foundations of the Mizo culture and offered an alternative way of life. Some characteristics are the absence of inter-village war and head hunting expeditions, subjection to the British authorities who often treated the common folk harshly, and even occasionally the chiefs, freed labour and many other new elements.[460] The Mizos became conscious of their ethnicity and their oneness of identity.[461] The introduction of Western education also greatly affected the life of the people in Mizoram. It was thought that Christianity led to the emergence of an "Elite group" or "privileged class."[462]

5.5. Relevance of the Study for Religion and Politics in Mizoram

The understanding of Church and State relations in Pauline epistles to Romans and Corinthians can throw light on the Mizo understanding of church and state relations in Mizoram. The concept of relations between the church and politics in the minds of the Mizo people is undoubtedly influenced by biblical writings. The present scenario of Mizoram politics is a real challenge to the Mizo Christians because of some confusion in thought with regard to Church and State relations. Therefore, this research intends to draw out certain implications from the previous chapters, which could be useful and applicable in the context of the Mizos as a whole.

---

[459] Ray, *Mizoram,* 17.

[460] Hrangkhuma, "The Mizos: A People Transformed by the Gospel,"13-14.

[461] Lalngurauva Ralte, "A Hundred Years of Christianity in Mizoram: Retrospective and Prospective," in *Ground Works for Tribal Theology in the Mizo Context* (RMCS 1; eds. Rosiamliana Tochhawng, K. Lalrinmawia & L. H. Rawsea; Delhi: ISPCK, 2007), 43.

[462] Lalrinthanga, *Church and State Relationship in the Mizo Socio-Political Life*, 57.

5.5.1. Strengthening the Idea of Identity Politics

The politically active Mizo elite are all Christians and hence in Mizoram Christians played a leading role in all the political development. It is believed that a majority of Mizo Christians believed that active participation in politics is not a Christian vocation rather it is a kind of unavoidable social service.[463] It is interesting to note that the Rising of 1966 known as *Rambuai*[464] was initiated by the Mizo Christians. In the meantime, the peace movement has been initiated by the church leaders, and the people who rejected the separation of the rebels were also Christians.[465] The Indian government suspecting Christian involvement in the rebellion or revolution has reinforced the negative mindset that Christians in the region are anti-national in the larger sense of Indian nationalism. As a result missionaries have gradually been removed from Mizoram and the whole of Mizoram is now classified as Restricted Area till today.[466]

The advent of the British form of Government marks the presence of political ideology in Mizoram. One of the political parties, the Mizo National Front (MNF)[467] revived the thought of the Mizo identity as their intention at that time of campaign was to preserve and safeguard Christianity in the face of challenges from hardcore

---

[463] R. Lalnunzira, "An Ethical Appraisal of Wolfhart Pannenberg's Concept of the Kingdom of God in Relation to the Understanding of the Kingdom of God Among the Mizo Christians," (M. Th Diss., Senate of Serampore College, 2008), 77.

[464] *Rambuai* refers to the armed rebellion for Independence in Mizoram from Indian Government, initiated by the underground Mizo National Front (MNF), broke out on 1st March, 1966. It was concluded with signing of the historic Peace Accord or Memorandum of Settlement, on 30th June, 1986, between the MNF and the Government of India. Margareth Ch. Zama, "The Role of the Church in Addressing the Issue of Peace in Mizoram," in *Ground Works for Tribal Theology in the Mizo Context* (RMCS 1; eds. Rosiamliana Tochhawng, K. Lalrinmawia & L. H. Rawsea; Delhi: ISPCK, 2007), 90.

[465] Hluna, *Church & Political Upheaval in Mizoram*, 19.

[466] Hluna, *Church & Political Upheaval in Mizoram*, 19.

[467] MNF was founded under the leadership of Laldenga on the 28th October, 1961.

elements of Hinduism and Islam. The MNF believed that the Mizos are a distinct nation, created, moulded and nurtured by God and nature.[468] Lalthangliana asserted that the Mizo people did not want to be dominated by Indians and the struggle for freedom was the result of their religious grievances[469] A reading of the life of the early Christians, aimed at safeguarding their religion and society which remains the need of the hour. Meanwhile, the Indian government like the Emperor and the Roman rulers blamed Christians as the traitors to the nations, and the Mizo Christians, who were involved in developing their own political ideology were seen as anti-national. But a lack of fear and unceasing attempts by the early Mizo freedom fighters shows us the light ahead and Mizoram is now known as a "Peaceful State" in India. Therefore, the politics of identity will bring back a sense of oneness and community if we interpret the context of the suffering Christians who were in the midst of different culture and ideologies.

5.5.2. Suppression of Divisions of Communities Within Party Politics

In the early days, the chief were given authority to interfere in the administrations under the jurisdiction of the superintendent. This was soon challenged by the emergence of a new elite group. Thus racial and political revolution started in Mizoram. The British administration, after carefully looking at the situation suppressed such political activities with a view to maintain status quo in their administration of Mizoram. Therefore, there was no organized political activity of any kind in Mizoram until the end of the Second World War.[470]

The political events brought by the Second World War brought a keen desire among the educated Mizo youths to organize themselves into political parties. Since they were totally excluded from the

---

468 Hluna, *Church & Political Upheaval in Mizoram*, 90.

469 Lalthangliana, Secretary, External Affairs (MNF), Government of Mizoram, Letter to Stanley Nichols Roy, General Secretary, APHLC, No. 20 (1) EA/66 dated Aizawl, the 13th March, 1967.

470 Hluna, *Church & Political Upheaval in Mizoram*, 62.

mainstream of Indian Nationalism, they could not accept their identity as Indian.[471] Soon after the British left India, a number of political parties started to appear. But the Mizo chiefs were unhappy as it could weaken their authority in the administration. Thus the anti-chief movement even took the form of mob violence causing physical harm to the chiefs and their followers. Thus, we find that from the beginning, great ideological differences between the parties began to appear within the Mizo communities. Therefore, there is a need for re-interpretation and application of Paul's teachings of the communitarian ideas in the context of Mizoram. The present scenario of Mizoram politics completely reveals that ideologies do not form political battle-fields because the actual battles were fought on smaller issues and sometimes between individual and personal issues.

5.5.3. Involvement of Churches in State Political Affairs

The Mizoram Presbyterian Church Synod has put in much effort for good governance in political affairs. The church, from the time of the MNF movement in the 1960s, has voiced a condemnation of violent activities in Mizoram which has been against the teaching of Gospels and the human rights as well. The Baptist Assembly of Serkawn endorsed the step taken by the Presbyterian Church, charging the MNF for the sufferings of the Mizo people.[472] Both the churches believed that there must be peace and security in Mizoram and have appointed representatives to deal with the matter. The issue was then discussed openly with the leaders of the political party and they resolved some issues.

H. T. Sangliana, a retired Police officer who has become a popular politician believes that the duty of all Mizo Christians is not to withdraw themselves from political affairs, but rather to give their best for the good governance of the state.[473] Lalsawma, a retired pastor of the Mizoram Presbyterian Church also suggested

---

[471] Hluna, *Church & Political Upheaval in Mizoram*, 63.

[472] Hluna, *Church & Political Upheaval in Mizoram*, 107.

[473] H. T. Sangliana, "Mizo Kristiante leh Politics," in *Kum 100 Kristian Zofate Hmabak* (Bangalore: Bangalore Mizo Christian Fellowship, 1994), 129.

that Mizo society should work for salvation in the form of Christian involvement in nation building. He further states that Christians should take part in nation building. He was against the statement that "Christians should not take part in politics."[474] Thus, the context of Romans 13:1-7 could have been interpreted among the Mizos in a very meaningful manner as many Mizo Christians are reluctant to involve themselves in politics and have no intention to support the government for the welfare of the people.

5.5.4. Church Prophetic-Witness Role to the State

The church involvement in politics is rarely welcomed by most political parties in Mizoram. However, the church has the firm idea that it should not keep away from politics for the sake of common good. Almost all the Churches in Mizoram are of the opinion that they should take the initiative to bring about political reforms and to make Mizoram free from corruption and other vices. One of the prophetic roles played by the Church in Mizoram in connection with political affairs is the institution of the *Mizoram People Forum.* The *Mizoram People Forum* came into existence on 21st June 2006 having Psalm 37:3 "Dwell in the land, and feed on faithfulness"[475] as its biblical basis. It was formed with various ecclesiastical denominations and non-government organizations (NGOs), at the initiative of the Mizoram Presbyterian Church (MPC). The main intention of this organization is to fight against injustice, financial corruption, and misuse of development funds and educate the people to have free and fair thinking.[476] H. S. Lalbiakiengi, in her article highlights some of the goals and objectives of MPF in a concise manner.[477] It is

---

[474] Lalsawma, "The Shaking Foundations in Mizo Society," in *Ground Works for Tribal Theology in the Mizo Context* (RMCS 1; eds. Rosiamliana Tochhawng, K. Lalrinmawia & L. H. Rawsea; Delhi: ISPCK, 2007), 67.

[475] Lalbiakmawia Ngente, *Mizoram People Forum: MPF Chanchin: 2006-2014* (Aizawl: L. B. Associates, 2016), 7-8.

[476] C. Lalhlira, "Institution of MPF for Political Reform," *PR* XI & XII (2005): 31.

[477] 1.To work towards establishing democratic government through free and fair election 2.To reform the electoral process and do away with the corruption and malpractices in the electoral system in the state 3.To put in place

interesting to note that the MFP played active role during the elections in Mizoram since 2006. They send letters to the Governor[478] and High Officials for free and fair elections and are against extravagance campaigns.[479] Pauline teaching of church and state relationship is seriously taken up by this Forum and significant changes could be seen as many political parties are trying to implement the above objectives imposed by the MPF.

5.6. Conclusion

Both church and state have their own responsibility in fulfilling their duties accountable to God and the people. The duty of the church is to support the State in fulfilling its function. Christians are called to transform the world in fulfillment of God's will. Though Christians are informed to obey the laws of the state, we should remember that the intention of the biblical writers is not a blind submission to the authorities. We are called to transform the state and society by attracting what is a contradiction to the teaching of the Bible. Sometimes, people have a conviction that church should not be involved in the political realm and politics should not intervene in the life of the church. Neglecting politics never makes people of the country good Christians. Rather, the church must be courageous to criticize the State and politics if found necessary in the light of the Gospel and the teachings of the Bible particularly in the Pauline teachings. Since the present political situation and

---

a transparent, accountable and responsible government 4.To educate the people on the governance issue and make them to be a responsible citizen 5.To guide and advise the government on developmental issues 6.To conduct the social audit for social reforms 7.To counter any form of violence, use of arms and terrorism. See H. S. Labiakengi, "NGO In Electoral Reforms of Mizoram: A Challenge," in *International Journal of Science and Research (IJSR).* https://www.ijsr.net/archive/v3i8/MDIwMTUzODk%3D.pdf. Accessed on 17th November, 2016.

[478] MPF Letters to the Governor of Mizoram Dated: Aizawl the 15th May 2008.

[479] Sangzuala Hmar, "Mizoram Polls sans Shine: EC, Church Serve Notice Against Extravagant Campaigns," *The Times of India* (14 October, 2008)), 6 See also Debash Dasgupta, "Divine Edict," *Out Look* (29 December, 2008), 33; Samudra Guptakashyap, "Poll with a Difference," *The Indian Express* (24 November, 2008), 13.

the State administration have been seen to go against the Christian teachings, this is high time the Mizo Christians to come out and get involved in politics for further extension of the Kingdom of God here on earth.

Chapter 6

Conclusion

This research has attempted to analyze church and state relations in Pauline undisputed letters from the context of the Greco-Roman world. Detailed studies of the first century context exposed that the Roman Empire have intimate relationship with the elites and the burgesses. The social and political life were also influenced and maintained by the high class people whereas the common people were in a vulnerable position in society. The Roman Imperial Theology brought glorification of the Roman state through the imperial cult as a religion was a response to power and prestige. *Pax et securitas/pax Romana* attracts people to be more submissive to the Roman state as it owed legal help and protection. The practice of the system of hierarchy in the Roman state wins the conquered people to become more submissive to the rulers and authorities. Moreover, patronage to the Roman emperor made life complex which resulted to creating barriers between the rich and the poor. The life of the early Christian community also witnesses divisions between the elite and the non-elite which implies inequality among the weak and the strong in the community.

Critical examination of the selected texts shows that the early Christians do not necessarily foster resistance, rather encourage people to live under the rulers with obedience and submission to the ruling authorities for the welfare of the state. Even some of the ruling authorities of the Roman Empire gave liberty to other religions until and unless they are under the colony of the Roman Empire. This shows that there is no idea of separation of church and religion in the early centuries as the Christians also enjoyed their privileged status. In the Mizoram context, when Christianity came to the soil, the first converts were urged by missionaries to separate religion from politics and were separated from traditional social life and activities. But at the same time, the missionaries enjoyed and supported the colonial power, whereas the new converts were faced with enmity mostly from the society at large and the chiefs in particular. This is due mostly to their reclusion from the social and community activities. This shows tension and separation of religion and politics in the mindset of the general populace However, as time passed, attitudes toward religion and politics also changed, and it dawned on the people that by combining the two tensions, improvements in political administration, positive growth could be attainable. Thus, it can be argued that the separation of religion and politics that began with Christianity's entry to Mizoram is one of the serious mistakes made by the Mizos.

Conflicts within Christian community at Corinth emphasizes the necessity of subordinating state as wisdom of God has to be motivating factors for the characters and minds of the Corinthian Christians. Dichotomy between religion and the secular is clearly seen in the lives of the people. The early Christians were influenced by the practices of the Roman laws and were more inclined to follow the Roman rules. The reason might be that the elite in the Corinthian community were tempted by individualism that led them to moral degradation and to widened gap between the rich and the poor. They exercised a number of unfair means in the judicial system of the first century. It can be observe that the Corinthians were simply acting as the elite had always done in Corinth. In Mizoram context, many politicians and governing authorities who are enrolled in church membership are believed to be involved in corruption, bribes and other form of malpractices which is contrary to the teaching of Christianity. Many Mizo Christians nowadays reluctant and withdrew themselves from creative involvement and contribution to shaping good governance as they tend to dismiss politics as unethical and irrelevant to Christian living. For them, politics is seen as a benefit and interest to few of the elite and the able persons. Therefore, it is an urgent need for the Mizo Christians to reform social and political life where both the rulers and the people should support each other in order to fulfill the mission of God on earth. As a good citizen of the country, politics is the place where we can come together to tackle issues of common concern for which we bear a collective responsibility. As Paul has suggested the Corinthian Christians to settle their problems among themselves, we are also called to challenge the problems that come into our politics and our society.

By looking into the present scenario of the Indian political system, strengthening the civil society is an urgent need as it will pave ways for involvement of the common people in State affairs. Civil society is to be seen as a useful instrument for the smooth functioning of the state. Sometimes, they raise a critical voice against the state but it becomes the voice of those who have no political authority. But this does not mean that they are in a position to oppose the state rather they are a voice of resistance against an ideology that could lead people into the condition of incapability and dysfunction. In Mizoram, in order to strengthen civil society, a number of NGOs were formed. They were committed to fight for certain specific issues and developed an alternative vision for the state. Of these, the contribution of The Mizoram People Forum (MPF), one of the most active agents of the NGOs is worth mentioning. Besides, a number of organizations are formed for active participation in building up good governance of the state. It is interesting to note that the church in Mizoram often extended its helping hand to the ruling government authorities in the form of exhortation and encouragement, and also sometimes constructive criticism for the good governance of the state.

Finally, the relation between religion and politics in India needs to be reflected on as many people especially lower castes witness exploitation and suffering from the government. The churches in India have a role to play and contributions to make for the welfare of the state. The mission of the church is to bring spiritual salvation of the people but at the same time demands the exercise of social responsibility which is to work in partnership with State and Civil Society to transform the evils of the world. At the end, this research does not attempt to provide a comprehensive solution for the involvement of Christians in politics. Rather, it tries to suggest how the church should influence and motivate the business of State for welfare of the citizens which is acceptable from the teaching of the Bible and those efforts that will be useful for the reformation of the socio-political life of India in general and Mizoram in particular.

Bibliography

I. Lexicons, Commentaries, Dictionaries and Encyclopedia

Aune, David. *Revelation.* Word Biblical Commentary 52A. Dallas, Texas: Word Books, 1997.

Barrett, C.K. *A Commentary on the Epistle to the Romans.* London: Harpers & Row, 1957.

__________. *The First Epistle to the Corinthians.* Black's New Testament Commentaries. Edition. London: A & C Black, 1968.

__________. *A Commentary on the First Epistle to the Corinthians.* London: Adam & Charles Black, 1976.

Bauer, W. *A Greek-English Lexicon of the New Testament and Other Early Christian Literature.*. 3rd edition. Translated by William F. Arndt and F. Wilbur Gingrich. Revised and edited by Frederick William Danker. Chicago: University of Chicago Press, 2001.

Bruce, F. F. *Romans.* Tyndale New Testament Commentaries. Grand Rapids, Michigan: Eerdmans, 2000.

Conzelmann, Hans. *A Commentary on the First Epistle to the Corinthians.* Philadelphia: Fortress Press, 1975.

Cranfield, C. E. B. *A Critical and Exegetical Commentary on Romans.* The International Critical Commentary. Edinburgh: T & T Clark, 1979.

__________. *Romans: A Shorter Commentary.* Edinburgh: T & T Clark, 1985.

Dunn, James D.G. *Romans 9-16.* Word Biblical Commentary 38b. Dallas: Word Books, 1988.

Edwards, James E. *Romans.* Understanding the Bible Commentary Series. Grand Rapids, Michigan: Baker Books, 1992.

Fee, Gordon D. *The First Epistles to the Corinthians.* Grand Rapids, Michigan: Eerdmans, 1988.

Fitzmyer, Joseph A. *Romans: A New Translation with Introduction and Commentary.* The Anchor Bible. New Haven and London: Yale University Press, 1993.

__________. *The Letters to the Romans.* The New Jerome Biblical Commentary. Bangalore: Theological Publication of India, 1999.

Heard, Warren. "Zealot." Pages 958-962 vol. 5 in *The New Interpreter's Dictionary of the Bible.* Edited by Katharine Doob Sakenfeld et.al.; Nashville: Abingdon Press, 2009.

Heim, K. M. "Kings and Kingship." Pages 610-623 in *Dictionary of Old Testament: Historical Books.* Edited by Bill T. Arnold & H. G. M. Williamson; Leicester, England: InterVarsity Press, 2005.

Horsley, Richard A. "The First and Second Letters to the Corinthians." Pages 220-245 in *A Postcolonial Commentary on the New Testament Writings.* Edited by Fernando F. Segovia and R. S. Sugirtharajah. London: T & T Clark, 2007.

Irwin, B. P. "Social Justice." Pages 719-734 in *Dictionary of the Old Testament Prophets.* Edited by Mark J. Boda & J. Gordon McConville; Nottingham, England: InterVarsity Press, 2012.

Kasemann, Ernst. *Commentary on Romans.* Grand Rapids, Michigan: Eerdmans, 1980.

Keck, Leander E. *Romans.* Abingdon New Testament Commentaries. Nashville: Abingdon Press, 2005.

Kittel, Gerhard and G. Friedrich. eds. *Theological Dictionary of the New Testament.* Translated by Geoffrey W. Bromiley. 10 vols. Grand Rapids, Michigan: Eerdmans, 1964-1976.

Metzger, Bruce M. *A Textual Commentary on the New Testament Greek*. England, London: United Bible Society, 1971.

Moffatt, James. *The First Epistle of Paul to the Corinthians.* London: Hodder and Stoughton, 1938.

Moo, Douglas. *The Epistle to the Romans.* The New International Commentary on the New Testament. Grand Rapids, Michigan/ Cambridge, U. K.: Eerdmans, 1996.

Morris, Leon. *The First Epistle of Paul to the Corinthians: An Introduction and Commentary*. Leicester: Inter-Varsity Press, 1958.

__________. *The Epistle to the Romans.* The Pillars New Testament Commentary. Grand Rapids, Michigan/Cambridge, U. K.: Eerdmans, 1988.

Mott, S.C. "Civil Authority." Pages 141-142 in *Dictionary of Paul and His Letters.* Edited by Gerald F. Hawthorne, Ralph P. Martin and Daniel G. Reid. Leicester, England: InterVarsity Press, 1993.

Moulton, Harold K. *The Analytical Greek Lexicon Revised.* Grand Rapids, Michigan: Zondervan Publishing House, 1978, 250.

Murray, John. *The Epistle to the Romans.* The New London Commentary on the New Testament. London: Marshall, Morgan & Scott, 1960.

Murphy-O Connor, Jerome. "The First Letter to the Corinthians." Pages 816-829 in *The New Jerome Biblical Commentary.* Edited by Raymond E. Brown, Joseph A. Fitzmyer and Roland E. Murphy; Bangalore: Theological Publications in India, 1999.

Neufeld, Dietmar. "Social Science: New Testament." Pages 300-310 in *The Oxford Encyclopedia of Biblical Interpretation.* Edited by Steven L. McKenzie; New York: Oxford University Press, 2013.

Orr, William F. and James Arthur Walther. *1 Corinthians: Introduction with a Study of the Life of Paul, Notes, and Commentary.* Garden City, New York: Doubleday & Company, Inc. 1976.

Sampley, J. Paul. *The First Letter to the Corinthians.* The New Interpreter's Bible. Nashville: Abingdon Press, 2002.

Sanday, William and Arthur C. Headlam. *A Critical and Exegetical Commentary on the Epistle to the Romans.* The International Critical Commentary. Edinburgh: T & T Clark, 1958.

Spurgeon, Andrew B. *1 Corinthians: An Exegetical and Contextual Commentary.* India Commentary on the New Testament. Bangalore: Primalogue Publishing Media, 2012.

Stuhlmacher, Peter. *Paul's Letter to the Romans.* Translated by Scott J. Hafemann. Edinburgh: T & T Clark, 1994.

Taylor, Mark. *1 Corinthians: An Exegetical and Theological Exposition of the Holy Scripture.* The New American Commentary. Tennessee, Nashville: B & H Publishing Group, 2014.

Whitelam, Keith W. "King and Kingship." Pages 40-48 in *The Anchor Bible Dictionary.* Vol. 4. New York: Doubleday, 1992.

Winter, Bruce, *1 Corinthians: New Bible Commentary.* Illinois: InterVarsity Press, 1994.

Witherington III, Ben. *Paul's Letter to the Romans: A Socio-Rhetorical Commentary.* Grand Rapids, Michigan/Cambridge, U.K.: Eerdmans, 2004.

__________. *Conflict & Community in Corinth: A Socio-Rhetorical Commentary on 1 and 2 Corinthians.* Grand Rapids, Michigan/ Cambridge, U.K.: Eerdmans, 1995.

Ziesler, John. *Paul's Letter to the Romans.* TPI New Testament Commentaries. Philadelphia: Trinity Press International, 1989.

II. Monographs

Achtemeier, Paul J., Koel B. Green and Marianne Meye Thompson, *Introducing the New Testament: Its Literature and Theology.* Grand Rapids, Michigan: Eerdmans, 2001.

Barrett, C. K. *The Epistle to the Romans.* London: Adam & Charles Black, 1971.

__________. *Essays on Paul.* Philadelphia: The Westminster Press, 1982.

Bell, Albert A. *Exploring the New Testament World.* Nashville: Thomas Nelson Publishers, 1998.

Blomberg, Craig L. *Jesus and the Gospels: An Introduction and Survey.* 2nd edition; Nashville, Tennessee: B & H Academic, 2009.

Bright, John. *History of Israel.* London: SCM Press Ltd., 1982.

Brown, Raymond E. *An Introduction to the New Testament.* Bangalore: Theological Publications in India, 2000.

Bruce, F. F. *1 and 2 Corinthians.* London: Oliphants, 1971.

Brueggemann, Walter. *Theology of the Old Testament: Testimony, Dispute, Advocacy.* Minneapolis: Fortress Press, 1997.

Carter, Warren. *The Roman Empire and The New Testament World: An Essential Guide.* Nashville: Abingdon Press, 2006.

Crocker, Cornelia Cyss. *Reading 1 Corinthians in the Twenty-First Century.* New York/London: T & T Clark International, 2004.

Cullmann, Oscar. *The State in the New Testament.* London: SCM Press, 1955.

Culver, Robert Duncan. *Towards a Biblical View of Civil Government.* Chicago: Moody Press, 1974.

Dev, Bimal J. and Dilip Kumar Lahiri, *Lushai Customs and Ceremonies.* Delhi: Mittal Publications, 1983.

Dodd, C. H. *The Epistle of Paul to the Romans.* London: Hazell Watson and Viney, 1949.

Dunn, James D. G. *The Theology of Paul the Apostle.* Grand Rapids, Michigan/ Cambridge, U. K.: Eerdmans, 1998.

Dutch, Robert S. The Educated Elite in the 1 Corinthians: Education and Community Conflict in Graeco-Roman Context. T & T Clark International, 2005.

Eichrodt, Waltger. *Theology of the Old Testament,* Vol. 1. London: SCM Press Ltd., 1960.

Elliott, Neil. *The Arrogance of Nations: Reading Romans in the Shadow of Empire.* Minneapolis: Fortress Press, 2008.

___________. *Liberating Paul: The Justice of God and the Politics of the Apostle*. Maryknoll, New York: Orbis Books, 1994.

Esler, Philip Francis. *Community and Gospel in Luke-Acts*. Cambridge: Cambridge University Press, 1987.

Ferguson, David. *Church, State and Civil Society.* Cambridge, U.K.: Cambridge University Press, 2004.

Ferguson, Everett. *Backgrounds of Early Christianity.* Grand Rapids, Michigan: Eerdmans, 1987.

Gerstenberger, Erhard S. *Theologies in the Old Testament.* Translated by John Bowden; Minneapolis: Fortress Press, 2002.

Hagelberg, Dave. *The Revelation of Jesus Christ to the Seven Churches and to Us Chapter 1-11*. Delhi: ISPCK, 2013.

Hengel, Martin. *Was Jesus a Revolutionist?* Translated by William Klassen; Philadelphia: Fortress Press, 1971.

____________. *Property and Riches in the Early Church.* London: SCM Press Ltd., 1974.

Hluna, John Vanlal. *Church & Political Upheaval in Mizoram.* Aizawl, Mizoram: Mizo history Association, 1985.

Hminga, Chhangte Lal. *The Life and Witness of the Church in Mizoram.* Serkawn: The Literature Committee of the Baptist Church of Mizoram, 1987.

Horsley, Richard A. *Jesus and Empire: The Kingdom of God and the New World Disorder*. Minneapolis: Fortress Press, 2003.

Horsley, Richard A. and John S. Hanson, *Bandits, Prophets & Messiahs: Popular Movements in the Time of Jesus.* Edited by Richard A. Horsley. San Francisco: Harper and Row Publishers, 1988.

Jeffers, James S. *The Greco-Roman World of the New Testament Era: Exploring the Background of the Early Christianity*. Downers Grove: Illinois: IVP Academic, 1999.

Johnson, Luke Timothy. *Among the Gentiles: Greco-Roman Religion and Christianity.* London : Yale University Press, 2009.

Kauppi, Lynn Allan. *Foreign But Familiar Gods: Greco-Romans Read Religion in Acts.* London : T & T Clark, 2006.

Keener, Craig S. *The Historical Jesus of the Gospels.* Grand Rapids, Michigan: Eerdmans, 2009.

Kim, Seyoon. *Christ and Caesar: The Gospel and the Roman Empire in the writings of Paul and Luke.* Grand Rapids, Michigan: Eerdmans, 2008.

Kipgen, Mangkhosat. *Christianity and Mizo Culture.* Aizawl, Mizoram: Mizo Theological Conference, 1997.

Koester, Helmut. *History, Culture, and Religion of the Hellenistic Age,* Vol. 1 in *Introduction to the New Testament.* Philadelphia: Fortress Press, 1982.

Lalchungnunga. *Mizoram: Politics of Regionalism and National Integration.* New Delhi: Reliance Publishing House,1994.

Lalnithanga, P. *Political Development in Mizoram.* Revised & Enlarged; Aizawl: P. Lalnithanga, 2006.

Lalpekhlua, L. H. *Contextual Christology: A Tribal Perspective.* Delhi: ISPCK, 2007.

Lalrinthanga, H. *Church and State Relationship in the Mizo Socio-Political Life: 1952-2006.* Delhi: ISPCK, 2013.

Lalsawma. *Revival: The Mizo Ways.* Aizawl Mizoram: Lalsawma, 1994.

Lalthangliana, B. *India, Burma & Bangladesh Mizo Chanchin.* Aizawl: Remkungi, 2001.

Lloyd, J. Meirion. *History of the Church in Mizoram.* Aizawl, Mizoram: Synod Publication Board, 1991.

MacMullen. *Romanization in the Time of Augustus.* New haven, CT: Yale University, 2003.

Malsawmdawngliana. *Negotiating the Past: Memory, History and Culture of Mizo.* Guwahati: Scientific Book Centre, 2015.

Matera, Frank J. *Romans.* Grand Rapids, Michigan, Baker Academic, 2010.

Meeks, Wayne A. *The First Urban Christians: The Social World of Apostle Paul.* New Haven and London: Yale University Press, 1983.

Morrison, Clinton. *The Powers That Be: Earthly Rulers and Demonic Powers in Romans 13:1-7*. London: SCM Press, 1960.

Nanos, Mark D. *The Mystery of Romans: The Jewish Context of Paul's Letter*. Minneapolis: Fortress Press, 1996.

Nolan, Albert. *Jesus Before Christianity.* Maryknoll, New York: Orbis Books, 2003.

Parry, N. E. *A Monograph on Lushai Customs and Ceremonies.* Assam: Assam Government Press, 1976.

Pearson, Birger Albert. *The Pneumatikos–Psychikos Termiology in 1 Corinthians.* Missoula, Montana: Scholars Press, 1973.

Powell, Mark Allan. *Introducing the New Testament: A historical, Literary, and Theological Survey*. Grand Rapids, Michigan: Baker Academic, 2009.

Ralte, Lalhruaitluanga. *Zoram Vartian: Chanchintha leh Thuziak Khaw Var Tan Dan*. Aizawl: Fineprints, 2008.

Ray, A. C. *Mizoram.* New Delhi: Ministry of Information and Broadcasting Corporation, 1972.

Rowland, Christopher. *Christian Origins.* London: SPCK, 1985.

Sampley, J. Paul. *Pauline Partnership in Christ: Christian Community and Commitment in Light of Roman Law*. Philadelphia: Fortress Press, 1980.

Sangkima. *Mizos: Society and Social Change: 1890-1047* .Delhi: Spectrum Publications, 1992.

Schnelle, Udo. *Apostle Paul: His Life and Theology.* Translated by M Eugene Boring; Grand Rapids, Michigan: Bakers Academic, 2003.

____________. *The History and Theology of the New Testament Writings*. London: SCM Press Ltd., 1998.

Schreiner, Thomas R. *Romans.* Grand Rapids, Michigan, Baker Academic, 1998.

Shakespear. *The Lushei Kuki Clans.* London: Macmillan and co., Ltd., 1912.

Stambaugh, John. and David Balch. *The Social World of the First Christians.* London: SPCK, 1986.

Stegemann, Ekkehard W. and Wolfgang Stegemann. *The Jesus Movement: A Social History of Its First Century.* Translated by O. C. Dean, Jr.; Minneapolis: Fortress Press, 1995.

Tenney, Merril C. *New Testament Survey.* Leicester, England: Inter-Varsity Press, 1985.

Thanga, Lal Biak. *The Mizos: A Study in Racial Personality.* Gauhati: United Publishers, 1978.

Thanzauva, K. *Theology of Community: Tribal Theology in the Making.* Aizawl, Mizoram: Mizo Theological Conference, 1997.

Thrall, Margareth E. *The First and Second Letters of Paul to the Corinthians.* Cambridge: Cambridge University Press, 1965.

Vanlalhluna, John. *Church and Political Upheavals in Mizoram.* Aizawl: Mizo History Association, 1985.

Vanlalchhuanawma. *Mission and Tribal Identity: A Historical Analysis of the Mizo Synod Mission Board from a Tribal Perspective: 1953-1981*. Delhi: ISPCK, 2010.

___________. *Christianity and Subaltern Culture: Revival Movement as a Cultural Response to Westernisation in Mizoram*. Delhi: ISPCK, 2006.

Weiss, Johannes. *Earliest Christianity: A History of the Period AD 30-150*, Vol. II. New York: Harper Torch-books, 1959.

Winter, Bruce W. *After Paul Left Corinth: The Influence of Secular Ethics and Social Change*. Grand Rapids, Michigan: Eerdmans, 2001.

Winter, Bruce W. *Seek the Welfare of the City: Christians as Benefactors and Citizens.* Grand Rapids, Michigan: Eerdmans, 1994.

Wright, N. T. *Paul and the Faithfulness of God.* Minneapolis: Fortress Press, 2013.

__________, *Paul: In Fresh Perspective.* Minneapolis: Fortress Press, 2005.

Yoder, John Howard. *The Politics of Jesus.* Grand Rapids, Michigan: Eerdmans, 1972.

Zawla, K. *Mizo Pi Pute leh An Thlahte Chanchin.* Aizawl: Lalnipuii, 2011.

III. Articles in Edited Books

Agosto, Efrain. "Patronage and Commendation, Imperial and Anti-Imperial." Pages 103-124 in *Paul and the Roman Imperial Order.* Edited by Richard A. Horsley; Harrisburg, PA: Trinity Press International, 2004.

Bammel, E. "Romans 13." Pages 365-384 in *Jesus and the Politics of His Day.* Edited by Ernst Bammel and C. E. D. Moule; Cambridge: Cambridge University Press, 1984.

Brown, John Pairman. "Techniques of Imperial Control: The Background of the Gospel Event." Pages 357-377 in *The Bible and Liberation : Political and Social Hermeneutics.* Edited by Norman K. Gottwald; Maryknoll, New York: Orbis Books, 1983.

Crossan, John Dominic. "Roman Imperial Theology." Pages 59-74 in *In the Shadow of Empire: Reclaiming the Bible as a History of Faithful Resistance.* Edited by Richard A. Horsley; Louisville, London: Westminster John Knox Press, 2008.

Carey, Greg. "The Book of Revelation as Counter-Imperial Script," Pages 157-174 in *In The Shadow of Empire: Reclaiming the Bible as a History of Faithful Resistance.* Edited by Richard A. Horsley; Louisville, London: Westminster John Knox Press, 2008.

Diehl, Judith A. "Anti-Imperial Rhetoric in the New Testament." Pages 38-81 in *Jesus is Lord, Caesar is Not.* Edited by Scot McKnight and Joseph B. Monica; Downers Grove, Illinois : IVP Academic, 2013.

Esler, Philip F. "Palestinian Judaism in the First Century." Pages 21-46 in *Religious Diversity in the Graeco-Roman World.* Edited by Dan Cohn-Sherbok and John M. Court; Sheffield, England: Sheffield Academic Press, 2011.

Gill, David W. J. "Acts and the Urban Elites." Pages 105-118 in *The Book of Acts in Its t Century Setting.* Vol. 2 of *The Book of Acts in Its Graeco-Roman Setting.* Edited by David W. J. Gill and Conrad Gempf; Grand Rapids, Michigan: Eerdmans, 1994.

Gottwald, Norman K. "Early Israel as an Anti-Imperial Community." Pages 9-24 in *In the Shadow of Empire: Reclaiming the Bible as a History of Faithful Resistance.* Edited by Richard A. Horsley; Louisville, London: Westminster John Knox Press, 2008.

Hminga. C. L. "The Traditional Mizo Concept of God." Pages 45-53 in *Towards Tribal Theology: A Mizo Perspective.* Edited by K. Thanzauva; Aizawl: Mizo Theological Conference, 1989.

Horsley, Richard A. "Introduction." Pages 1-24 in *Paul and the Roman Imperial Order.* Edited by Richard A. Horsley; Harrisburg, PA; Trinity Press International, 2004.

Horsley, Richard A. "Conclusion." Pages 177-182 in *In the Shadow of Empire: Reclaiming the Bible as a History of Faithful Resistance.* Edited by Richard A. Horsley; Louisville, London: Westminster John Knox Press, 2008.

Hrangkhuma, F. "The Mizos: A People Transformed by the Gospel." Pages 3-15 in *Ground Works for Tribal Theology in the Mizo Context.* Readings in Mizo Christianity Series 1; Edited by Rosiamliana Tochhawng, K. Lalrinmawia & L. H. Rawsea; Delhi: ISPCK, 2007.

Lalrinmawia, K. "Pialral Theology: Mizo Expression of Theology." Pages 142-153 in *Ground Works for Tribal Theology in the Mizo Context.* Readings in Mizo Christianity Series 1; Edited by Rosiamliana Tochhawng, K. Lalrinmawia & L. H. Rawsea; Delhi: ISPCK, 2007.

Lalsawma, "The Shaking foundations of Mizo Society." Pages 61-67 in *Ground Works for Tribal Theology in the Mizo Context.* Readings in Mizo Christianity Series 1; Edited by Rosiamliana Tochhawng, K. Lalrinmawia & L. H. Rawsea; Delhi: ISPCK, 2007.

Massey, James. "Inter-Play of Religion, Politics and Communalism in India." Pages 1-12 in *Inter-play of Religion, Politics and Communalism.* Edited by Samson Prabhakar; Bangalore: BTESSC/SATHRI, 2004.

Nystrom, David. "We Have No King but Caesar: Roman Imperial Ideology and the Imperial Cult." Pages 23-37 in *Jesus is Lord, Caesar is Not.* Edited by Scot McKnight and Joseph B. Monica; Downers Grove, Illinois : IVP Academic, 2013.

Oakes, Peter. "A State of Tension: Rome in the New Testament." Pages 75-91 in *The Gospel of Matthew in Its Roman Imperial Context.* Edited by John K. Riches and David C. Sim; London/ New York: T & T Clark International, 2005.

Pazawna, C. "Christianity in Mizoram: Vision for the Twenty-First Century." Pages 48-60 in *Ground Works for Tribal Theology in the Mizo Context.* Readings in Mizo Christianity Series 1; Edited by Rosiamliana Tochhawng, K. Lalrinmawia & L. H. Rawsea; Delhi: ISPCK, 2007.

Pixley, George V. "God's Kingdom in the First-Century Palestine: The Strategy of Jesus." Pages 378-393 in *The Bible and Liberation: Political and Social Hermeneutics.* Edited by Norman K. Gottwald; Maryknoll, New York: Orbis Books, 1983.

Ralte, Lalngurauva. "A Hundred Years of Christianity in Mizoram: Retrospective and Prospective." Pages 39-47 in *Ground Works for Tribal Theology in the Mizo Context.* Readings in Mizo Christianity Series 1; Edited by Rosiamliana Tochhawng, K. Lalrinmawia & L. H. Rawsea; Delhi: ISPCK, 2007.

Sangliana, H. T. "Mizo Kristiante leh Politics." Pages 118-134 in *Kum 100 Kristian Zofate Hmabak.* Edited by R. L. Rinawma, Tlanghmingthanga and Zaihmingthanga; Bangalore: Bangalore Mizo Christian Fellowship. 1994.

Thanzauva, K. "Introduction." Pages 1-8 in *Toward a Tribal Theology: The Mizo Perspective.* Edited by K. Thanzauva; Mizoram: Mizo Theological Conference, 1989.

Towner, Philip H. " Romans 13:1-7 and Paul's Missiological Perspective: A Call to Political Quietism or Tranformation?" Pages 149-169 in *Romans & The People of God.* Edited by Sven K. Soderlund & N. T. Wright; Grand Rapids, Michigan: Eerdmans, 1999.

Zairema, "The Mizo and their Religion." Pages 31-44 in *Toward a Tribal Theology: The Mizo Perspective.* Edited by K. Thanzauva; Mizoram: Mizo Theological Conference, 1989.

Zama, Dr. Margareth Ch. "The Role of the Chruch in Addressing the Issue of Peace in Mizoram." Pages 90-97 in *Ground Works for Tribal Theology in the Mizo Context.* Readings in Mizo Christianity Series 1; Edited by Rosiamliana Tochhawng, K. Lalrinmawia & L. H. Rawsea; Delhi: ISPCK, 2007.

IV. Journals

Biakmawia, C. "Biblical Resources for Christian Participation in Politics." *Mizoram Theological Journal* XI & XII (2005): 2-25.

Borg, Marcus "A New Context for Romans." *New Testament Studies* 19/2 (1973): 205-218.

Bruce, F. F. "Paul and the Powers that Be." *Bulletin of the John Ryland University Library of Manchester* 66 (1984): 78-96.

Dhanaraj, D. "The Bible and the State: The Church and the Indian Scenario." *Bangalore Theological Forum.* XXXIX/1 (2007): 142-160.

Fuliga, Jose B. "Church-State Relations and Civil Disobedience." *Asia Journal of Theology* 1/2 (2007): 475-477.

Gale, Herbert M. "Paul's View of the State: A Discussion of the Problems in Romans 13: 1-7." *Interpretation* VI/4 (1952), 409-414.

Illathuparampil, Mathew. "Church and Politics." *Jeevadhara* XXXVI/216 (2006): 479-493.

John, V. J. "The Role of the State in Jesus' View." *Bangalore Theological Forum* XXXVI/1 (2004): 1-18.

Kallas, James. "Romans XIII. 1-7: An Interpolation." *New Testament Studies* 11/4 (1965): 365-373.

Kroger, Daniel. "Paul and the Civil Authorities: An Exegesis of Romans 13:1-7." *Asia Journal of Theology* 7/2 (1993): 344-366.

Lalhlira, C. "Institution of MPF for Political Reform." *Presbyterian Review* XI & XII (2005): 31.

Lewis, Lloyd A. "The Law Courts in Corinth: An Experiment in the Power of Baptism." *Anglican Theological Review* 11 (1990): 88-98.

McDonald, J. I. H. "Romans 13:1-7: A Test Case for New Testament Interpretation." *New Testament Studies* 35 (1989): 540-549.

Mitchell, Alan C. "Rich and Poor in the Courts of Corinth: Litigiousness ans Status in 1 Corinthians 6:1-11." *New Testament Studies* 39 (1993): 562-586.

Stein, Robert H. "The Argument of Romans 13:1-7." *Novum Testamentum* XXXI 4 (1989): 325-343.

Winter Bruce W. "Civil Litigation in Secular Corinth and the Church." *New Testament Studies* 37 (1991): 559-572.

V. Newspaper and Letters

Dasgupta, Debash. "Divine Edict." *Out Look* (29 December, 2008), 33.

Guptakashyap, Samudra. "Poll with a Difference." *The Indian Express* (24 November, 2008), 13.

Hmar, Sangzuala. "Mizoram Polls sans Shine: EC, Church Serve Notice Against Extravagant Campaigns." *The Times of India* (14 October, 2008)), 6.

Lalthangliana, Secretary, External Affairs (MNF), Government of Mizoram, Letter to Stanley Nichols Roy, General Secretary, APHLC, No. 20 (1) EA/66 dated Aizawl, the 13th March, 1967.

MPF Letters to the Governor of Mizoram Dated: Aizawl the 15th May 2008.

VI. Webliography

H. S. Labiakengi, "NGO in Electoral Reforms of Mizoram: A Challenge." *International Journal of Science and Research (IJSR). https://www.ijsr.net/archive/v3i8/MDIwMTUzODk%3D.pdf.* Accessed on 17th November, 2016.

Mizoram Religion Census 2011 *http://www.census2011.co.in/data/religion/state/15-mizoram.html* Accessed on 7th February, 2017.

VII. Unpublished Thesis

Lalnunzira, R. "An Ethical Appraisal of Wlofhart Pannenberg's Concept of the Kingdom of God in Relation to the Understanding of the Kingdom of God Among the Mizo Christians." M. Th Diss., Senate of Serampore College, 2008.

Renthlei, Lalmuanawma. "The Concept of 'King' and 'Kingdom' in John's Gospel: Implications for Religio-Politics Relationship in Mizo Context." M. Th Diss., Senate of Serampore College, 2016.